BUSINESS MENTORING
SUCCESS

HOW TO BUILD A WORLD-CLASS
MENTORING BUSINESS

STEVE HACKNEY

Foreword by
Brendan Purcell

BUSINESS MENTORING SUCCESS
HOW TO BUILD A WORLD-CLASS MENTORING BUSINESS

ISBN 978-0-9567907-5-0

Published in the UK by TCA Publishing

TCA
PUBLISHING

DEDICATION

To Pete, Rob, Julia, and our entire team... I couldn't have done this without you. You'll never know how much I appreciate and love you all.

To my wife, Helen, who has been a rock throughout my rugby-playing days and my business career. I love you so much.

To my amazing children, Thomas, Matthew and Liv... you drive me each day to be a better person, dad and mentor!

And to the hundreds of business mentors we help and support around the world... you ensure we never get complacent and keep pushing the bar higher and higher.

TABLE OF CONTENTS

ACKNOWLEDGEMENTS

I consider myself to be extremely lucky in terms of my sporting and business careers. Not because of what I've achieved, but in terms of the mentors that took the time, understanding, patience and commitment to help me navigate through all the challenges that sport and business throw up. Without them all, I would never have scaled the heights I did playing rugby union nor achieved so much as a business mentor and, now, 'mentor' to business mentors around the world.

No one can ever 'make it' in this world without the help of others. I've been so fortunate to have been supported by a number of truly remarkable people. It's true that at the time I don't think I really appreciated the help and advice I was getting from those below, but I am grateful beyond words.

First, I want to focus on my sporting mentors...

When I arrived at Loughborough University in 1987, I was so fortunate to have Jim Greenwood as my tutor. Jim, you were way ahead of your time, and your ground-breaking books *Think Rugby* and *Total Rugby* are still relevant today. I remember playing for a Micky Steele-Bodger XV against Oxford University in 1987 at Iffley Road, and I played a blinder. All the national press were eulogising about me and how "Redbrick Downs Oxford" (*The Times*)... but, despite all the compliments, one of the reports explained that "his try-scoring feats made you forget about Hackney's defensive frailties". The day after, you summoned me to your office and asked me what went wrong! We dissected every missed tackle, and you put a plan in place for me to ensure it never happened again. I was never a great tackler, but after that day and the work we did together, there weren't many people who got past me. You are sorely missed Jim... and I never got chance to really thank you for all you did for me whilst I was at Loughborough.

My time at Nottingham RFC was memorable for many reasons, particularly our off-field antics, but, most importantly, Alan (Davies), you took me under your wing as a fresh-faced 19-year-old and made me a better player, as you did with everyone you worked with. You were destined to coach the national team for Wales; I just wish you had been blessed with a vintage team. Sadly, you weren't. When I told you I was thinking of leaving Nottingham for Leicester Tigers, you invited me to your home, and we spent the next four hours putting the pros and cons down for whether I should stay or go... and then when I told you I was leaving, you wished me all the best. You'll never know how difficult that decision was.

Joining Leicester Tigers was pivotal in me meeting many incredible sporting and business mentors. First, Tony (Russ), you too were ahead of your time. You were the world's first paid rugby union coach, and even though we were amateurs at the time, you completely transformed how we trained. We became professional in every way, other than being paid! Much of the preparation you put in place was unseen outside of the club, but you took a struggling and under-performing team and transformed us into champions. You were instrumental in me joining the club. You painted me a picture of what success would look like... and I was joining a team that already had three *international* players in my position (Rory and Tony Underwood, and Barry Evans – one of the BIG 'cons' on the list that Alan and I wrote down), and whilst you obviously didn't give me any promises, you said that if I worked hard and played well, I would get a fair chance. So, 170 games and 86 tries later, and I think it's fair to say you were true to your word!

The club replaced Tony Russ, after we had just won the league title, and appointed Bob Dwyer... the legendary 1991 coach of World Cup winners Australia. The goal was for Bob to build a team that would dominate Europe and embrace professionalism (rugby union turned professional in 1995 just after the World Cup).

Bob, I'll never forget the first day we were formally introduced to you. The squad, along with all our wives, partners and girlfriends, were assembled in the Hilton Hotel just off junction 21 of the M1 motorway), and after greeting all the players and our partners by name, you went on to tell us we were not as good as we all thought! You said our basic skills were nowhere near good enough (in the room there were rugby legends such as Martin Johnson, Dean Richards, Joel Stransky, Will Greenwood, Rory Underwood, Eric Miller, Austin Healey, Richard Cockerill, Neil Back, Darren Garforth, Graham

Rowntree, and so on!). You taught us all the value and the importance of basic disciplines, and that it's not 'practice makes perfect' but 'perfect practice makes perfect'. And, whilst many people won't see this or agree with me, what you put in place in those early years paved the way for the club to be the most successful English club over a 20-year period. I learned so much from you, Bob.

And last but by no means least, Sir Clive (Woodward)... I only played for you once, against Argentina. But there was no doubt you would win the World Cup for England. You were an inspiration to me back then and still are. You were one of the first to take what you had learned in running a successful business and apply it to elite sport. You took a very amateur England setup and transformed it kicking and screaming into a world-class environment, one that I aspire to every day when working with our business mentors.

My first business mentor was Pat Costello. You were only four years older than me, Pat, but you were the first person to teach me about selling (we were selling Canon photocopiers!). You took what were effectively kids with no sales experience and transformed us into a formidable sales team. You loved 'rugby lads', because you knew we had a good work ethic, although with me, Martin Johnson, Aadel Kardooni (both Tigers legends), Richard Davison (rest in peace, Rich) and Stuart Maxwell all in one office, that must have been one hell of a challenge to keep us all in step! But you did. You guided me through my formative years in industry, and you laid the foundation for my success today. Thanks, Pat.

After selling photocopiers I joined P&G Bland, a large commercial insurance broker (and now part of Oval, a huge insurance group). Peter Wheeler and Les Cusworth, both rugby legends, were, respectively, my Managing Director and Sales Director. It may sound like it was 'jobs for the boys', but it wasn't! We had to work hard every day. Remember, back in 1992 rugby union was still an amateur sport, and we didn't earn a bean for playing, so the career was important financially. Pete and Les, you showed me both the value of working hard and the importance of having fun at work, too. And boy did we have fun! You were both considerate with the amount of time I needed off for rugby, and we formed a very successful team, outperforming all the other divisions in the company for three years straight.

During my time at Bland's I was introduced to Jim Saker. Jim was running the School of Business and Economics at Loughborough University and is now Director of the Centre for Automotive Management at the University. Jim worked with me without any remuneration to help me raise £2.3 million to build one of the new stands at Welford Road. It was obviously a huge project and daunting for me, but, Jim, you guided me through the whole process. Your marketing nous, your amazing support and your insights became the foundation of much of my work today. I will always be indebted to you, Jim. Thank you.

When I then transitioned into running my own businesses (after rugby turned professional) many people have been amazing mentors to me, and none more so than Richard Brewin. Rich, you taught me so much about running a successful business and the importance of 'knowing the numbers'. You are always willing to help, and I can't thank you enough for the support you've given me professionally and as a friend over the years.

I can say, without question, that the mentoring, support and guidance I've received from all of you has been absolutely instrumental in helping me and the hundreds we help to create world-class and highly successful mentoring businesses.

Thank you.

FOREWORD

By Brendan Purcell

(Performance Director of British Rowing)

I met Steve on the side of a freezing rugby pitch. Xander, my son, and Matthew, Steve's son, were both playing for Nottingham Rugby Club Under 14s. Because we had so much in common, both in sport and business, Steve and I quickly became good friends. It therefore gives me great pleasure to write the foreword for *Business Mentoring Success*.

At the time I first met Steve, I was the Performance Director at British Triathlon, where I oversaw the success of our Olympic and Paralympic teams on the world stage.

My team and I led Great Britain to seven medals at the Rio 2016 Olympic and Paralympic Games, including an historic second Gold for Alistair Brownlee and a first-ever medal for a British woman for Vicky Holland. In the inaugural Paralympic triathlon, Great Britain finished second in the medal table, with one Gold, two Silvers and one Bronze.

I am currently the Performance Director for British Rowing, one of the largest Olympic sports in terms of medals across all disciplines.

Prior to that, as an athlete I competed on the world stage in canoeing for Australia and, after retiring from competitive sport, I first worked with Australia's high-performance canoeing and diving programmes before moving to the UK, joining the GB canoe sprint programme prior to the 2008 Olympic Games. I was appointed Head Coach to the canoe sprint team after the Beijing Games, leading the programme during its most successful Olympic cycle.

So, like Steve, I enjoyed success at an elite-athlete level and, subsequently, in our careers as coaches and mentors.

I've always had a scientific approach to coaching world-class athletes. In my time with British Triathlon and now with British Rowing we analyse biometric data (data produced from the technology we use to measure literally dozens of different psychological and physical parameters), not simply in terms of race and athlete performance, but in plotting a pathway for the athletes and the sport to thrive.

I'm constantly looking for ways to give our coaches, mentors and athletes a competitive edge. If we just continue to do what we have always done, we simply 'stand still'.

We have to make sure that we are staying ahead of the game, because the challenge that I've seen is that after a successful period of the last six Olympic Games, a lot of other countries are thinking, "If Great Britain can do it, we can do it". We have to stay ahead of that and challenge ourselves.

To ensure this, we use a three-pronged approach; we use scientific data to provide a figure to be compared and used to inform, working alongside experiential understanding and the importance of gut instinct.

But ultimately, performance on the water is what predicates the outcome.

That's why Steve's work in the boardroom and my work on the water is so similar.

Steve teaches that to create a world-class mentoring business you need to build it scientifically using a proven set of time-tested parameters and then supplement this with leading-edge tactics and strategies that produce results for the mentor and their clients.

We use a very similar philosophy. As I mentioned earlier, my team of coaches, mentors and experts use our three-pronged approach when working with our athletes to improve their performance and produce winning results.

My team of coaches and mentors has to be world class, otherwise we simply won't get world-class and improved results from our athletes. We therefore have two performance systems: one for our coaches and mentors, and one for our athletes. Both systems work in tandem to develop world-class coaches and mentors, and world-class athletes, resulting in world-class performances from everyone concerned.

As you'll see, as a business mentor, Steve recommends that you create a mentoring system for you and an implementation system for your clients. I can tell you it's this dual approach that has served my teams of coaches, mentors and athletes so well, and it will do the same for you, too.

The similarities between elite sport and building a world-class mentoring business are numerous. The epicentre of everything we do is to get improved results and performances for our athletes. That is the yardstick we are measured against, and it's the same for you.

If getting results for your clients is your primary objective, then you can focus everything else around it.

Business Mentoring Success will give you the exact blueprint in order to do this. Enjoy!

WHY BUSINESS MENTORING?

In case you are wondering *why* business mentoring is a viable path for you to take, I thought I'd take just a few minutes to explain why I believe it's one of the most rewarding, fulfilling and lucrative industries in the world.

Most, if not all, of the most successful business owners and entrepreneurs across the world have business mentors working alongside them. The likes of Steve Jobs (founder of Apple), Richard Branson (founder of Virgin), Bill Gates (founder of Microsoft), Bob Iger (Chairman and CEO of Walt Disney) and many more credit their business mentors with helping them achieve much of their success.

According to recent research carried out by Kabbage, Inc., a global financial services, technology and data platform, 92% of small business owners surveyed said that they believed business mentors would have a direct impact on the growth and development of their business, and 89% of business owners who didn't have a mentor wished they did.

It's hard to find more research on the business mentoring sector, but our own experience is probably the best litmus test for the market. We are one of the largest business mentoring organisations in the world, and what follows is fact and not based on research or small sample sizes (which, inevitably, leave questions unanswered).

The SME business sector is, of course, huge, irrespective of the country you reside in. Our business mentors and I typically work with small and medium-sized businesses, although we have worked with the likes of Xerox and other large businesses. However, and contrary to popular belief, in my experience if you get your mentoring service and your fees right, then the small and medium-sized business sector is very fruitful, and they have a huge appetite for working with business mentors.

As an organisation, we have a thriving community of hundreds of independent business mentors around the world. They work with thousands of business owners. Just over 92% of clients fall into the small business category (up to 50 employees). They pay our business mentors at least four hundred pounds, dollars or euros per HOUR. Yes, *per hour*.

And remember, these are small businesses. Very few other business mentors command this level of fees, but this book has been written to explain EXACTLY how you can tap into the world's largest business sector and charge at least four hundred pounds, dollars or euros per hour as a business mentor.

But as you know, for anyone to be fulfilled, it's not just about how much money you make, and this is why being a business mentor ticks many boxes.

From a personal point of view (and I know most of our business mentors feel the same way), there's nothing better than helping other people reach their goals and aspirations. Even small 'wins' should always be celebrated. As a business mentor, your clients wouldn't be able to achieve their results without your help, support and guidance. Without you, many of them get 'lost' in their business. They genuinely don't have anyone else to talk to about their business. It can be a very lonely place being a business owner and entrepreneur, and that's one of the big reasons why business mentoring is such a growth industry.

Perhaps one of the reasons why having a business mentor is so important for so many people is that it gives them accountability. It ensures they get stuff done. It therefore ensures their business is improving all the time, even if you have to drag them kicking and screaming!

Then, of course, there's the sense of personal achievement. Even the small wins are joyous. I'll give you a simple example of what I mean...

My mentors and I focus on growing a client's business. We're *Business Growth Mentors*. One of the simple and easy-to-implement tactics we ask a business owner to employ right at the beginning of the relationship is to send their clients, customers or patients a simple letter: the 'Testimonials by the Dozen Letter'. This is a one-page letter (results are far better when it's sent as a letter rather than an email) sent by the client to their customers. Its purpose is simple: it urges their clients, customers or patients to send written or video testimonials about how great they are as a business.

You see, very few businesses have great testimonials from their clients, customers or patients. The letter is written in such a way that the response rates are very high. Often, over 50% of customers will respond with either a written or video testimonial. Imagine the impact on the business owner and their team when they get a flood of great testimonials from their customers? It's uplifting for them and without question results in the business being able to acquire more clients, customers or patients than ever before because of the *proof* they've just assembled. The sense of personal achievement my mentors get from seeing the testimonials come in and the client being so excited is pure gold!

Many of our business mentors join our community because they are tired of extensive business travel or because their work–life balance isn't great. As a business mentor, you can work from home. Because of the amazing advancement of the internet and all the apps and tools you can use, you don't even have to visit your clients to have your meetings (like I used to have to do). You can use any online meeting platform such as Skype, Zoom or GoTo Meeting.

You can structure each day and each week around what YOU want. You decide. Being a business mentor gives you complete flexibility on how you live your life.

There are many more benefits of being a business mentor, but, to be brutally frank, the simple fact is that most business mentors aren't consistently successful in terms of clients and results. Nor have they figured out how to build a successful business tailored to their personal requirements (financially and their needs and wants).

That's what you'll get from reading this book. And as you entrust me to guide you through the process, I promise never to give you any BS or theory, just everything that works.

WHAT IS BUSINESS MENTORING SUCCESS?

Business Mentoring Success is basically a proven **blueprint** to take what you know and apply it to another person's business by MENTORING.

The word 'mentoring' conjures up many different meanings. This description, in my mind gets it spot on...

> *Mentoring is most often defined as a professional relationship in which an experienced person (the mentor) assists another (the mentee) in developing specific skills and knowledge that will enhance the less-experienced person's professional and personal growth.*

Key to the entire process of mentoring is that the mentor must have a skill set which the mentee doesn't possess, otherwise little or no commercial and personal growth will occur.

Like many things, it's not 'what you do' that's important; it's *'how you do it'* that counts.

...and, believe me, having been a business mentor in many forms since 1997, I can tell you most people don't get it right. In my experience, the vast majority of business mentors (and business coaches) struggle day in, day out to make a good living, despite the fact that they really do have skills and knowledge above and beyond many business owners.

Of course, just having a skill set and knowledge base that business owners don't have, does NOT guarantee success!

What you have to do is become astute and expert at selling your mentoring services to the right people; those who can afford your services and remain your clients for many months, even years. Key to this is having a mentoring service that not only delivers results to your clients, but also maximises your fees and minimises the time you work with them, thereby giving you the capacity to work with dozens, even hundreds of clients.

But it's even more than this...

The US TV star and entrepreneur Oprah Winfrey said...

> *"A mentor is someone who allows you to see the hope inside yourself."*

I completely agree.

Always remember, you're not providing *just* mentoring services... you're providing a vehicle for the business owner, your client... to believe that you can help them... to give them hope... to give them direction and the realisation that what they want to achieve can be achieved, especially (ideally, *only*) with your help. When you can do that, you're on the fast track to creating a wonderful mentoring business.

Business Mentoring Success will take you by the hand and explain (and show you) exactly what you need to do to achieve all of these things.

Most people haven't figured this out.

Yet business mentoring is one of the fastest-growing industries on the planet. If you want to get started in business mentoring, or if you want to add it as another lucrative income stream, then *Business Mentoring Success* will give you a proven blueprint for how to do it... and do it without making the myriad of mistakes (many of them costly) I've made and many more people are making right now.

INTRODUCTION

It was the summer of 1999. A couple of months earlier I had decided to hang up my rugby boots for good (most people thought I should have done so years earlier!). I'd been steadily growing my business, Hackney Marketing, since rugby turned professional in 1995, in the hope that once I did retire from playing rugby, I could seamlessly transition from elite sportsman to successful business owner.

In the main, that plan worked, but I was far from being what you could call a successful business owner at this point. Anyway, for the first time since I was 16 years old, I was able to go on holiday without having to train every day. I could have a beer at lunchtime and eat whatever I wanted. This was going to be some holiday! Thomas, our first child, was 4 years old, so my wife Helen had booked us into a very nice child friendly hotel in Majorca.

Before leaving for the holiday I had set up a couple of meetings... one with a potential client and the other with an existing client, so I was looking forward to having a fantastic holiday, followed by a great start to working 100% on my business.

Well, it *was* a great holiday. I drank and ate to my heart's content, and my feet didn't see a pair of trainers for a full two weeks!

We returned home on the Sunday night, and I was looking forward to the next day and my two meetings. I didn't know this at the time, but that fateful Monday would become a very significant day with respect to my mentoring business and where I am today.

I woke bright-eyed and bushy-tailed the next morning, and then I encountered my first challenge on 'civvy street': I'd partied so much on holiday that I couldn't get my suit trousers fastened!

That was a complete shock to say the least. I'd never ever encountered that before. I'd been on a strict training regime since I was 16, and this was the first time ever that I had put weight on in the wrong areas.

However, I managed to take three deep breaths and just about fastened the button on my trousers, but it was very uncomfortable. Nevertheless, I was early to my first meeting.

But it was terrible.

I went there to sell my mentoring service, which was based around helping the business owners grow their business, but they couldn't grasp how I could help them and why it would 'cost' so much. I told them it wouldn't 'cost' them anything if they worked with me, because of the money I'd help them make. I told them about my amazing feat of generating £2.3 million for the shiny new stand at Leicester Tigers and explained the success I was having with some of my clients. I told them I knew there were gaps in their sales and marketing that I could help them fix. But they weren't having any of it. They definitely wanted to grow their business… but I wasn't going to be the person to help.

I was perplexed.

But they just didn't get it, which is what I always used to say to myself if someone didn't work with me: 'They just don't *get* it' (more on this later).

As I was about to leave, the owner of the business said something that's never left me… "Steve, I have no doubt you could help us, but there doesn't seem to be any structure to your mentoring programme. I was looking for someone with a logical step-by-step system. I like you, but your service just looks a bit ad hoc". My initial reaction was to brush it off as an excuse, but later that day when I reflected on what he said, his criticism was the catalyst to creating something special (more on this shortly).

But my day wasn't finished.

I had a short drive over to my mentoring client's business. In the six months I'd been working with Julie I'd got to know her well. She ran a logistics consultancy company. In other words, her business helped large organisations move their 'stuff' from one place to the next in the quickest and most economical way. She worked with a number of the large supermarkets here in the UK.

As soon as I walked into her office I knew something was up. After the normal pleasantries, she just said it… "Steve, I've enjoyed working with you these past six months, but it's not working out. I want to CANCEL."

Those four words are every mentor's and coach's nightmare.

There's not a lot you can do once a client has said those four words ("I want to cancel"). There's no going back. I remember thinking to myself this is turning out to be a great first day (not!)

I asked Julie why she wanted to cancel, and this is what she said... "Steve, whilst I can see progress, it's been six months, and we have no tangible results to show for it."

Just remember that. It's key to building a world-class mentoring business.

So, it wasn't the best day I'd ever had, and I was genuinely upset. My initial instinct was to blame the prospect and the client, but deep down I knew it was all my fault.

Don't get me wrong; I had done some good things when growing my fledgling mentoring business. And in my experience many mentors and coaches do some good things, but they don't address exactly what the client wants and needs.

The next six months were painful for me, because I was 100% focussed on my business, and 100% reliant on the income it generated. I was able to dissect everything I did. I used the feedback from clients and prospects and decided to completely change how I worked.

For example, I discovered through painful experience that the following things must be addressed if you're going to create a world-class and highly successful mentoring business...

- Business owners have to 'believe' you can get them the results they seek.
- You have to demonstrate a method of working that sounds logical to them.
- Your mentoring service has to be affordable.
- You cannot just turn up. You have to have a mentoring SYSTEM.
- You cannot 'wing it'. They will eventually find you out.
- Clients ALSO need an implementation SYSTEM so they can apply what you advise on your mentoring calls.
- Your mentoring service has to be geared to get results early in the relationship.
- You need to position yourself away from all your competition.
- You need a way to acquire mentoring leads, not only during working hours but also while you sleep.
- You need a system for converting those leads into mentoring clients at the RIGHT fee.
- You have to have a way of working that allows you to work with dozens of clients on a one-to-one basis without it taking too much time.
- To accelerate your business faster, you also need a one-to-many mentoring programme.

There are others, but this book provides the solutions to these key elements. I'm also going to reveal all the other tactics you can use to help you build a world-class mentoring business.

I've learned a lot over the last twenty-plus years. I've probably made more mistakes than any other business mentor on the planet, and I (and my company) now work with hundreds and help thousands of business mentors across the world.

...and I still mentor clients myself. I work with only five clients (I don't have time to work with any more than that because of my commitments to our business mentors). I still work with clients, because firstly, I love doing it, and secondly, I don't want to put myself in a position where you or any of my business mentors can ever turn round to me and say, "Steve, what do you know? This may have worked 15 years ago but not now!"

You can therefore be 100% confident that what I reveal in this book is working right now... not twenty years ago! Of course, much of what you're about to learn is timeless and will work as well as it does now in 100 years.

In short, what follows is a blueprint anyone can use to create a world-class mentoring business that brings you the rewards you seek. That's my promise to you.

Okay, that's enough of an introduction. Let's get started...

CHAPTER 1:

WHAT DOES 'WORLD-CLASS' REALLY MEAN?

Before we get into detail, I first of all want to talk about actually being 'world-class'. As you know, I was fortunate enough to have a career in elite sport. I've also worked with sporting and business mentors who all strived to be world-class in whatever they did. Here's a great story to emphasise this point...

In 1996 we progressed to our first-ever European Cup Final which, unfortunately, we lost (although the club has won it twice since), but on the way to the knockout stages we were drawn away to a French club called Pau in the Pyrénées-Atlantiques. Like ours, their team was full of stars, and it was going to be a tough game with a partisan, raucous and quite intimidating crowd at their 18,000-capacity Stade du Hameau.

I have to say, in all my career, I'd never felt so pressurised by the crowd. Even our substitutes had to leave the stand towards the end of the game because of the intimidation. Imagine that... eight huge, 'ugly', battled-hardened rugby players being scared by supporters! Anyway, it became fiercely intimidating, because for most of the match we were behind, and in the last minute Leon Lloyd scored a stunning breakaway try to win the game. The crowd all thought there was a forward pass (there was no video ref back then!) so went crazy when the ref awarded the try.

I never thought we'd lose any game we played. Even with a minute left, I still believed... And I know my teammates felt the same.

It was an amazing win, and, as French clubs always do, despite the fact they lost, they put on a great after-match function!

One thing led to another, and we were all the worse for wear the next morning. We turned up for training, and Bob Dwyer, the coach, sat us all down and gave us all a right rollicking. He said, "we sat down at the start of the season and all agreed we wanted to become a world-class team, right? World-class doesn't just mean world-class on the training park and in matches. It means in EVERYTHING you do. Going out after a match and getting pissed, irrespective of the win, isn't world-class, is it?"

Fair point. Well made. And 100% right. We never did party like that again (only after winning a trophy, which was allowed!)

The New Zealand All Blacks are probably the best sporting team ever. Much of that stems from their world-class ethics. For example, when they're on tour, and they are obviously using training rooms provided by their hosts, at the end of the day, no matter how hard they train, they leave the training rooms as immaculate as they found them.

That's world class.

When you get your car serviced and you get a call the next day from the garage making sure everything is okay with your car. That's world class.

When you're never late for a meeting, whether that's in business or in your personal life... that's world class.

When you say you're going to do something for anyone, and you do it on time... that's world class.

When you put the results of your clients before everything else... that's world class.

When you send a thank-you note to a new client... that's world class (more on this later).

When you turn up for all your meetings well prepared... that's world class.

When you endeavour to be the best version of yourself every day... that's world class.

When you give the mentoring industry the respect it deserves (more on this later)... that's world class.

When you're prepared to give before you get... that's world class.

When you're with your partner, or your children, or your clients, or your friends, you give them absolutely 100% of you

(you don't answer calls or look at your email or scroll through your social media accounts)... that's world class.

And so on!

So, if you're building a mentoring business, why build an 'average' mentoring business... or a 'good' mentoring business? Why not strive and dedicate yourself to building a 'world-class' mentoring business?

Because standards are so low these days, it's so easy to stand out (we'll talk more about this later). If you aim to build a world-class mentoring business, even if you don't quite get there, it will look and feel like a world-class business to everyone else, because most other people do things so badly or 'averagely'.

Why not make the commitment right now that you are going to be driven by world-class standards?

I tell you this: just shifting your thinking from where you are now to having a world-class ethos will in itself transform your life and your business. And let's face it, it's not difficult. You just have to live and breathe world class. Sure, you won't be world class all the time – it's impossible to be perfect – but the closer you get to it, the closer and closer you'll be to getting everything you ever wanted out of your life and your business.

...and the best thing is, as you'll soon discover, *it's not rocket science!*

Chapter Summary

- Being world class is a state of mind.

- Anyone can make the commitment to run a world-class mentoring business. It takes no extra skill or knowledge. Just a shift in mindset.

- Why set up an 'average' or 'good' mentoring business, when you can create a 'world-class' mentoring business with little extra effort.

CHAPTER 2:

IT'S NOT ROCKET SCIENCE... BUT IT IS A SCIENCE

One very important lesson I've learned over the last twenty years or so is that building a mentoring business isn't rocket science, but it IS a science.

What does that mean?

To explain this using another sporting analogy, let me take you back to my rugby-playing days. The biggest asset to my game was my speed. I could run 100 metres in 10.6 seconds. That's not international class sprinting, but it's fast, and even today there aren't that many rugby players across the world who can run that fast.

Thing is, I knew the faster and more powerful I got, the better player I'd be. In fact, back in the 1990s, I held the speed record over 30 metres in all the England rugby training camps. But that didn't happen by chance. I was blessed with speed, but I worked tirelessly to improve. Central to my development were two experts in their fields. The club provided me and the other players with Merv Wilson. Merv was an outstanding speed coach and way ahead of his time. He was the first athletics coach (I believe) to have developed a unique technique called 'over-sprinting' using bungee ropes (I'll explain, don't worry!).

He was a mechanic by trade, and at the time it was well-known that if you could get the body to run faster than humanly possible in normal conditions, then the body would adapt to the extra speed and 'learn' to run faster. An example of that would be to run down a hill. And this was common practice with sprinters across the world. Trouble was, it was extremely dangerous and not easy to find the right hills that would enable the body to run faster for sustained periods. Nevertheless, it was a proven coaching drill.

So Merv had an idea. He took a twenty-metre piece of bungee rope and fixed both ends to a weight training belt. He would then get two of us to work together. He would stand the front person twenty metres down the track and attach the front weight training belt around their waste. And then the second person would be twenty metres behind with the other weight training belt around their waist.

Since the bungee rope was twenty metres long the rope was taught between the two people. He would then get us both in a sprint start position and would then say, "set... go!" That was the trigger for the front person, who would sprint as hard as they could, but of course as each step was taken the rope was getting tighter and tighter, making it tougher and tougher to move forward, so they were working on power, driving hard down the track. Then Merv would shout 'GO!' This was the trigger for the second person, who by this time was struggling to stay still because of the extra force being applied by the bungee rope getting tighter and tighter as the athlete at the front was moving forwards away from them. Of course, when the person at the back started to sprint the flex in the bungee rope would propel them faster than they could normally sprint (hence 'over-sprinting').

It was amazing... and it worked.

In short, it was the science of sprinting that Merv applied to make us run faster. It was genius.

But when you play rugby, it's not just about speed. There are many other facets that are important. But, for me, if I could match my increased speed with agility (i.e. the ability to beat opposition players at high speed), then I'd have a potent mix. Of course I was agile, but I knew I could get better. Enter Tim Exeter. Tim was, and still is, one of the world's best speed and agility coaches. He's worked with premiership football clubs such as Chelsea, many world-class rugby clubs, Formula 1 drivers, and so on (one time I asked him how on earth he could help Formula 1 drivers, and he said, well if I can get them to change gears using their paddles one hundredth of a second faster each time, then in the course of a race that will amount to several seconds, which then made complete sense!)

Anyway, I trained with Tim twice a week and paid for his services out of my own pocket. But it was worth it. I even had to drive to his home, which was 50 miles away!

Tim's whole philosophy was simple... the more you train the body on agility skills, the more agile and faster you'll get. He applied the science of speed and agility using a number of drills, and the result would be assured. Of course, it worked!

The point I'm trying to make with both these sporting examples is that both Merv and Tim simply followed the science of speed and agility. They developed systems and drills that, with practice, would improve the speed and agility of the people they worked with.

None of this is rocket science (i.e. hard to do), but it IS a science.

And what I've learned over the years is that building a mentoring business is EXACTLY like that. As long as you apply the science I reveal in this book, your mentoring business <u>will</u> be successful.

To be more specific, let me break down the elements required to create a successful mentoring business. These are the primary things you need to get right if you are to build a world-class mentoring business...

Because growing your mentoring business IS a science, let me show you how it looks as a simple equation. Take a look at figure 2.1...

$$R \times M \times L \times A \times M$$

$$=$$

Successful Mentoring Business

Figure 2.1

It's Not Rocket Science, but It IS a Science

There are just five elements you have to get right. They are...

R: Results for Your Clients

M: Mentoring Attraction Package

L: Lead Generation

A: Acquiring Clients

M: Maximising Client Value

...and the next five chapters will explain how you apply each one scientifically to your mentoring business...

Chapter Summary

- Growing a world-class mentoring business isn't rocket science, but it IS a science!

- Follow the Business Mentoring Success Equation:

$$R \times M \times L \times A \times M$$

$$=$$

Successful Mentoring Business

- The next five chapters cover each element of the success equation.

CHAPTER 3:

RESULTS FOR YOUR CLIENTS

$$\underline{R} \times M \times L \times A \times M$$

When I created my first business, Hackney Marketing, in 1995, it wasn't originally a mentoring business; it was a consulting business... or that was the plan. I didn't really know about business mentoring or coaching back then (not many people did!), but several years after retiring from playing rugby the business ended up primarily being a mentoring business for all the reasons I mentioned earlier.

I started and built the business like most other consultants did and still do. I was at the centre of my business, and everything I did was for the benefit of me. Sure, I wanted clients to do well, but it was about ME, first and foremost. At the time, I thought that made complete sense. But let me tell you a true story that instantly made me change my entire philosophy...

Even though my business had been steadily improving, it wasn't making the leaps I had envisioned. Back then I was working with about a dozen consulting clients, but results were sketchy to say the least. Some clients were getting good results, others not. That meant I was losing clients, like Julie who I mentioned earlier, because they weren't getting results.

The problem was that I didn't have a robust SYSTEM that produced predictable high-quality results... with every client.

Worse still, because of that, I was working differently with each client, and even though I'd repeat certain tactics and strategies that worked with other clients but, in effect, I was reinventing the wheel with every client. That's just plain stupid... but, of course, I didn't know any better back then.

I knew things had to change. I therefore looked at each client I had ever worked with and wrote down everything that produced results. I looked at my own business and wrote down everything that worked. I then put it all into a logical system that I could use that would hopefully produce predictable results for every client. I called it the *POWER Marketing System* (see figure 3.1 for a diagram showing the first two parts of the system).

So, to cut a long story short, it worked extremely well. Not only did I use it as my initial consulting system, over time, I developed it into my mentoring system and also packaged it and sold it as a step-by-step system that business owners *could implement themselves*. I sold it in 46 different countries.

So why was it so successful?

Three words... **it produced RESULTS**.

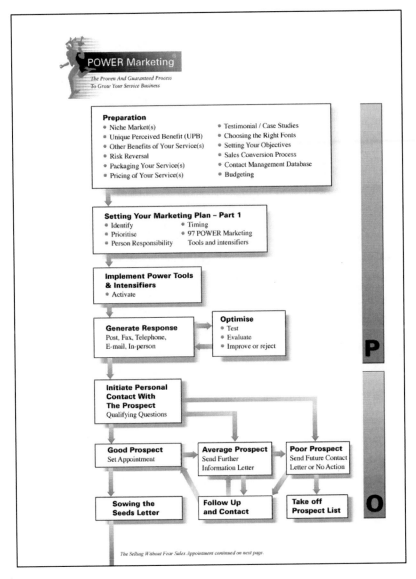

Figure 3.1

From that day forward, my entire philosophy on building a mentoring business changed. I knew that delivering results for clients had to be the key focus, because if you get clients the results they seek, then they will genuinely love you for it, pay you handsomely for it, and stay with you for many months, even years.

The POWER Marketing System has since developed into a system I call 'The FORMULA'. This is the results-producing system my mentors and I use when working with clients to produce predictable results for them.

The point I'm making here is that if you FIRST focus on your mentoring service to deliver predictable results for your clients, then what follows will take care of itself.

Without being able to help your clients get results, the rest of what follows in this book is irrelevant. IT HAS TO BE THE FOUNDATION OF EVERYTHING YOU DO. Achieve that, and I promise getting clients, retaining them and making a lot of money for you and your clients is doable.

Don't fall into the common trap of thinking that just because you have a skill set or area of expertise that your clients don't, then when you work with them it will produce predictable AND consistent results. I can tell you, it won't!

What you must do – and I implore you to do this – is to create a results-focussed mentoring SYSTEM that you can use with EVERY client.

You see, when you do this, it makes your life so much easier. You're not having to reinvent the wheel with every client.

You can tweak and improve each element of the system to suit and, better still, once it's in place you know it will help produce consistent results.

It gives you massive CONFIDENCE, too.

Now, we, of course, don't live in a perfect world, so the likelihood is that you'll need to develop your system as you're working with clients. But that's okay. Just have the mindset that you'll put your system in place as soon as you can.

I'd also like to say at this point, that most people DON'T START with a results-producing system for clients. They focus on generating leads and getting clients and worry about the results later. Instead, if you follow my approach, it will ensure that generating leads, acquiring clients, getting clients to pay you handsomely and retaining clients for a long time will be so much easier to do. This was life-changing for me!

But how do you create your own mentoring system?

I'm taking for granted you've identified an area of expertise or a skill set you have that business owners require... or you're willing to learn a different skill (which is completely doable – more on this later).

Here are the three categories of mentoring for business owners. They are...

- **CATEGORY 1: Business Growth**

  This includes the likes of sales and marketing, profit improvement, cost reduction, accounting and finance, customer service, etc.

- **CATEGORY 2: Business Infrastructure Development and Change Management**

  Human resources and staff recruitment, office selection and relocation, product or service production, information technology, logistics, operations, purchasing, legal, etc.

- **CATEGORY 3: Personal Development** (in relation to the business owner or owners)

  Health, fitness, well-being, diet, spiritual health, relationships, mental health, money, career development, goals, etc.

Basically, if your expertise can either help the business or the business owner(s) then you CAN become a successful business mentor, providing you follow the steps laid out in this book.

But first, as I said, you need to build your 'Mentoring System'.

Remember, having a successful, proven mentoring system in place... one you can rely on for every client... means you can deliver your mentoring service in the same organised and structured way with everyone, regardless of their differences... and achieve predictable, successful outcomes each and every time.

This really is a fundamental principle when it comes to building your mentoring business. You cannot hope to achieve outstanding results and grow your business rapidly if you're forever making things up.

As I explained before, your system brings consistency, and consistency breeds success... it's that simple.

Let me take you through the steps you need to take to create a step-by-step mentoring system.

Here's my six-step Mentoring System Template (M.S.T)...

Creating Your M.S.T

STEP #1: Map Out the High-Level Stages of Your System

A 'stage' is a key part of your system.

For example, stage 1 is likely to be your initial welcome call just after someone joins your mentoring programme.

Stage 2 will be your first mentoring call... and so on. Just create a high-level view of the system, identifying all the key stages.

That gives you your structure.

For example, figure 3.2 shows our Sales Accelerator Programme, the mentoring system our mentors deliver to their clients, and as you can see it has four high-level stages.

It doesn't matter how many high-level stages your system has.

It could, for example, be three or 17.

However, in most cases, it's likely to be fewer than 10.

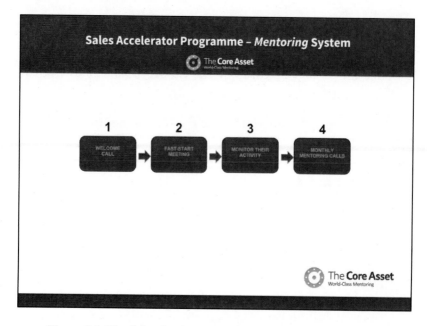

*Figure 3.2: The Sales Accelerator Programme – Mentoring System
(showing the four high-level stages)*

STEP #2: Add the Timeline to Deliver Each Stage

Next, you need to add the time it takes to deliver each high-level stage along with the timeframe between each.

This is important, because it defines the time required for each stage to be delivered and also the time delay between each stage.

To give you an illustration, figure 3.3 shows the timeline for our Sales Accelerator Programme. Notice that I've defined both the time required for each stage and the time delay between each stage.

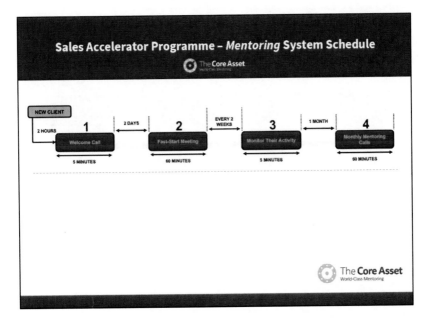

Figure 3.3: The Sales Accelerator Programme – Mentoring System
(showing the timeline)

STEP #3: Identify Deliverables

Next, you need to look at each high-level stage one by one and write down the deliverables or outcomes you're looking to achieve for each.

For example, a deliverable could be a demonstration of a tactic or strategy, an agreement to move to the next stage in your system or an action taken by the client.

Simply write down all the deliverables you want to accomplish at each stage.

Figure 3.4 shows the deliverable list of the Sales Accelerator Programme. As you can see, each stage has its own set of deliverables...

Stage #	Objective(s)
1. Welcome Call	1. Reassure the client that they have joined a professional organisation that delivers on its promises. 2. Arrange Fast-Track Meeting.
2. Fast-Start Meeting	1. Demonstrate how good The Core Asset Vault is. 2. Client fully aware of how to use The Core Asset vault. 3. Set client targets for next 12 months.
3. Monitor Their Activity	1. Keep track of the client's Core Asset Vault activity. 2. Encourage client to keep active.
4. Monthly Mentoring Calls	1. Keep the client on track. 2. Encourage the client. 3. Agree implementation for the next month.

Sales Accelerator Programme – *Mentoring* System
DELIVERABLES LIST

The **Core Asset**
World-Class Mentoring

Figure 3.4: The Sales Accelerator Programme – Mentoring System (showing the deliverables/outcomes)

Let's have a quick recap...

You've now got your system shown in a group of high-level stages. You've added the timeline to each stage and the duration between each, and you've defined the outcomes for each stage. Next is step 4...

STEP #4: Create the Step-by-Step Process

Now take each high-level stage in turn and create a step-by-step process for delivering the outcomes you've defined in STEP #3.

You should write this down as a series of steps (just as I'm doing here!).

The steps simply guide you through delivering all the outcomes for each individual stage.

Having done this, you now have the structure in place for each stage to ensure you deliver the identified outcomes.

For example, figure 3.5 shows the high-level stages and steps of the Sales Accelerator Programme.

STEP #5: Define and Detail Each Step

Next, take each step in each stage and define exactly what needs to be done to deliver each individual step.

For example, stage 2 of the Sales Accelerator Programme is the 'Fast-Start Meeting'. It has four steps.

At this point, I want to urge you to be very detailed in your explanation of what you're doing at each step.

The best way to think about this is to write each step as though someone completely new in your business is going to deliver the mentoring system.

Sales Accelerator Programme Mentoring System **3**
Introduction 3
STAGE 1: Welcome Call **4**
Introduction 4
STEP 1: Call The Client & Arrange The Fast-Start Meeting 4
STEP 2: Send Confirmation Email With Agenda 5
STAGE 2: Fast-Start Meeting **5**
Introduction 5
STEP 1: Text The Client 6
STEP 2: Prepare & Get Yourself Ready 6
STEP 3: Phone Client If Not Received Contact Request 7
STEP 4: The Fast-Start Meeting 7
STAGE 3: Monitor Their Activity **11**
Introduction 11
STEP 1: View The Client's Activity After The First Week & Then Every Two Weeks 11
STEP 2: Send Email After 1 Week 11
STEP 3: Send Email In Between Monthly Mentoring Calls 12
STAGE 4: Monthly Mentoring Calls **12**
Introduction 12
STEP 1: Email The Client 48 Hours Before The Call With The Agenda 12
STEP 2: View Their Activity In The Core Asset 13
STEP 3: The Mentoring Call 13
STEP 4: Scientific Marketing Makeover 13
The Scientific Marketing Makeover System **13**
Introduction 13
STEP 1: Select The Marketing Piece To Makeover 14
STEP 2: Complete The DNA Analysis 14
STEP 3: Move The DNA Thermometer Highlight Box To The Correct Thermometer 15
STEP 4: Complete The Improve The DNA Of The Core Elements Section 15
STEP 5: Review, Check & Save Ready To Present To The Client 16
STEP 6: Present Makeover To The Client 16
Lifelong Client **16**

Figure 3.5: The Sales Accelerator Programme – Mentoring System (showing the steps in each high-level stage)

This will make it easier for you to deliver the system as close to perfection as you can get whilst always realising you'll never reach perfection. It also means you're putting the framework in place to scale your business should you wish to do so, whereby you can bring in more business mentors to deliver your mentoring service to clients (don't let this pass you by).

Before moving on, I want to talk about your 'mentoring meetings'.

Whatever you call them, your 'meetings' are the time you spend with your client to deliver your mentoring service.

I used to meet my clients face to face. In the late 1990s and early noughties, I didn't really have a choice. The internet was still in its early stages, and bandwidth was still terrible. Using video for meetings was not possible.

Therefore, I had to drive to my client's office or, perhaps, we'd meet halfway. Whilst there are advantages to meeting face to face with your clients, one HUGE disadvantage is that it takes time to travel to and from each meeting. Plus, it's so much harder to conclude meetings on time when you meet face to face.

Ultimately, this meant I was wasting a serious amount of time simply travelling to meet clients.

But, now, we're so lucky. We don't have to do this. For example, our mentors and I conduct all our meetings with clients using an online meeting platform (Skype, Zoom, GoTo Meeting, WebinarJam, etc.).

It means you don't waste a single minute. You can meet your clients in the comfort and safety of your home or office and not have to move an inch.

And because the technology is so good now, it's virtually like meeting your clients in person.

I currently have a mentoring client in Germany, one in the US, one in Australia and two in the UK. Having that mix of clients wouldn't have been doable 15 years ago. Now I conduct all my mentoring calls online, and it's been transformational. It's the same for our mentors.

You should do this, too.

You still, of course, need to prepare for them.

For example, you should make sure if you're at home that your 'environment' is professional in all regards. You should instruct your family or anyone else at home that you're not to be disturbed. Put a lock on your door if possible... and, of course, dress using the right attire, and so on.

There's an hilarious clip on YouTube showing what can happen if you're not fully prepared.

It shows eminent expert, Professor Robert Kelly being interviewed live on BBC News about South Korea. But he makes the mistake of not locking his door and his two children end up coming into his office, swiftly followed by his wife.

It's like a take from a sitcom!

The screenshot shown as figure 3.6 shows his two children in the background.

Figure 3.6: Professor Robert Kelly and his two young children gate-crashing his live interview on BBC News (he obviously didn't read this book!)

Now, whilst this is hilarious, it's not something you want to happen whilst carrying out your mentoring meetings!

You've been warned...

And, to finish on this, don't even think of meeting your clients face to face.

You lose nothing meeting them using an online meeting platform and, as long as you make it clear right at the start of your relationship that this is how you work, no client will have an issue with it. I accept there may be, in exceptional circumstances, a valid business case to attend in person (for example to 'pitch' to an assembled Board meeting for substantial additional business), but you should, of course, only commit to do so as a special case and agree to budget for it accordingly!

A huge benefit of this approach is that it means there are NO LIMITS to WHERE your clients come from.

Therefore, I urge you to consider only online mentoring meetings with your clients. Agreed?

STEP #6: Create Templates

Finally, you need to create the document templates required for each step within each stage.

For example, create any emails you would need to send to the client and agendas for each meeting contained in that particular step.

Here's an email and figure 3.7 shows the agenda template we use prior to the Monthly Mentoring Calls at stage 4 in our mentoring system...

Subject: Our Monthly Sales Accelerator Mentoring Call...

Hi First name of client,

I hope you're okay and everything is going well.

Please find attached the Agenda for the mentoring call we have scheduled in a couple of days.

Let me know if there's anything else you'd like to talk about and I'll add it to the agenda.

Speak soon.

Kind regards,

Name

Business Growth Mentor

Sales Accelerator Programme
Monthly Mentoring Call
Agenda

DETAILS:			
Company Name:	Enter client's business name	**Attendees:**	Client's name and Your name
Date of Meeting:	Enter date of meeting	**Time:**	Start and finish time (45 mins)

1. Review of last month
2. Is there anything you need extra help with?
3. Scientific Marketing Makeover
4. Progress so far against the targets set
5. Next month actions
6. Tune in to Steve's next ACCELERATE webinar
7. Questions?
8. Arrange next month's mentoring call

ACTIONS	WHO?	WHEN?

- 1 -
Sales Accelerator Programme - Monthly Mentoring Call Agenda

The Core Asset
World-Class Mentoring

Figure 3.7: The Sales Accelerator Programme – Mentoring System (showing the 'Monthly Mentoring Call Agenda')

At this point let me just quickly mention the importance of having clear and succinct agendas.

You may think sending an agenda in advance is 'old hat', but I can assure you this is as important now as it was 20 years ago. All world-class businesses use agendas. They have a number of important benefits...

- They demonstrate to the client that you're professional and organised (isn't that what you want your clients to think of you? Well agendas do that and require zero skill).

- They keep your mentoring meetings focussed and on track.

- They ensure you never get 'lost' in the process.

- Whoever creates the agenda has the 'power' (positions you as a 'leader'). Again, isn't that what you want your clients to think of you?

- They ensure each meeting has a set of actions to be taken care of (usually by the client).

...and that's how you create a bullet-proof mentoring system for your business that will help you deliver an outstanding mentoring service that gets results for clients and gets you ready to scale if and when you decide to do that.

But you're not finished yet.

To complete the loop you actually need two systems!

Having a mentoring system for yourself puts you into the top 10% of business mentors. However, what I'm about to tell you now, as long as you act on it, will put you in the top 1% of business mentors.

But before I jump in. Let me tell you a story...

As I mentioned, I originally didn't have any system at all. I then developed the POWER Marketing System (shown previously). I would mentor clients through each stage of the system. Each mentoring call would focus on a specific section (in order) of the system. For example, if we had progressed to applying 'Risk Reversal', then the mentoring call would focus on how the client would create a risk reversal strategy (guarantee) in their business. They'd take notes (although not all of them did), and after around an hour the meeting would end. Clients always loved those meetings, because they were learning things that they didn't really know. So, everything was positive... but it was pretty much downhill *after* each meeting.

Now don't get me wrong, a few business owners could take what we discussed and create the tactic or strategy to a decent level, but the majority couldn't. That meant that a couple of days after the mentoring meeting I'd get a call or an email from the client asking more questions about the tactic or strategy we discussed. I'd then have to spend time re-explaining. And this would go on and on. Therefore, the hour your client is paying for, isn't really an hour, is it? It could be two hours with the additional phone calls and email exchanges. This essentially halved my mentoring fee, and it will do the same for you if you let it! For example, if you charge £400 a month, which is for one hour of your time a month, you've gone from making £400 an hour to £200 an hour. Not good. Worse still, you've just reduced your available time by an hour, meaning you won't be able to take on as many clients or use that time in other ways more productively.

You see, what happens after your mentoring meeting is that the client then goes back into their business, and wherever they pick up, it once again consumes them. They get immersed in the daily grind of running their business, so when they get around to working on the tactic or strategy you discussed, they forget much of what you told them. Secondly, in most cases the business owner won't have implemented the tactic or strategy before, so it's always going to be a struggle for them. That means their results won't ever be great... which in turn means your effectiveness as a business mentor is diminished.

This scenario is played out every day across the world and explains why business mentors and coaches struggle to get results with clients and therefore why it's a constant battle to keep hold of them.

No matter how amazing your meetings are with your clients... no matter how good you are as a business mentor... I can assure you the outcome in almost every case will be as I've just described.

So, what's the solution?

Well, it's obvious to me now, but back then it certainly wasn't. Having a mentoring system for you to guide your client through isn't enough. It is, of course, vital, but what you need is an IMPLEMENTATION SYSTEM *for the client* that dovetails into your system.

In its simplest form, your implementation system is basically a set of 'How To' guides created for the client relating to every tactic or strategy in your system.

So, if you talk about tactic 'A' at the end of the meeting, you hand the client the 'How to Implement Tactic A'... and so on.

By doing this, you...

- reduce the number of emails and calls from the client wondering what to do, thus maintaining your fees and not eating into your time;

- give the client a step-by-step blueprint for creating and then implementing the tactic, making it so much easier for them;

- significantly increase the chances of the tactic being more effective once implemented;

- vastly improve your clients' satisfaction with you and your mentoring service.

My advice is to start with simple, step-by-step 'How To' guides. Write each guide in the format of Step 1... Step 2... Step 3... and so on.

You can break down any tactic or strategy into bite-sized steps.

Then, once you've created the 'How To' guides for all your tactics and strategies, look to add the following (making it even easier for the client and increasing their competence and results)...

- Checklists

- Templates

- Video overviews

To illustrate, figure 3.8 shows you an example 'checklist' and figure 3.9 shows you the 'template' for creating powerful 'Headlines', which is one of the tactics we discuss with our clients (Headlines are very important for increasing the response and sales in every marketing tactic, like web pages, order forms, letters, ads, emails, and so on).

These additional elements will take you time to produce but will be more than worth it. Remember, you only have to create them once. You then use the same documents for EVERY client.

You should then take it a step further and create a 'membership' website. In simple terms, your membership website is a repository for all your 'How To' guides and supplementary documentation and videos. The site should be password protected, and as soon as you acquire a client, you simply give them access to it. Your own membership site is the icing on the cake and once again puts you in the top 1% of business mentors.

And if you're worried about the technical aspect of building a membership site, you needn't.

There are a number of excellent solutions you can use where the application makes it relatively easy for you to create your own membership site.

We use two different platforms. For our mentors we use Click Funnels ($297 per month)...

www.clickfunnels.com

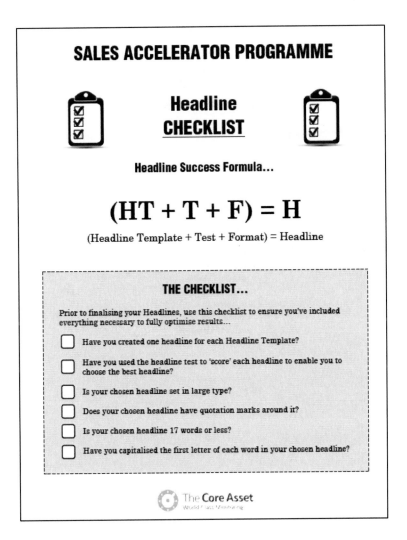

Figure 3.8: Example 'Checklist' for creating powerful headlines

SALES ACCELERATOR PROGRAMME

Headline

Headline Creation Template

PLEASE NOTE: It is highly likely that you will use a different headline for each marketing strategy you use (each page on your website, subject line of emails, print ad, leaflet, Google AdWords, etc.). Therefore, you should follow the process below for creating your headline for **each** marketing strategy you use...

NAME OF MARKETING STRATEGY: _____

Headline Element	Use The Following	Your Headline
(HT) Headline Template	Use the following templates... How To... Benefit Headline 2- or 3-word headline Quick & Easy Solution Warning Headline Testimonial Headline Reasons Why Headline Offer Headline Write at least one headline for each template in the space provided.	

The **Core Asset**
World Class Mentoring

Figure 3.9: Example 'Template' for creating powerful headlines (showing first page)

The Click Funnels platform enables you to build a simply structured membership site, and it will be more than adequate for you.

The other leading membership site builder is called Kartra...

www.kartra.com

Both Click Funnels and Kartra offer many other benefits in addition to helping you build a professional membership site, and I'll cover this in more detail later.

For our clients' membership site, we use an application called Umbraco.

Our web developer put this membership site together for us. We needed much more functionality for clients than the 'off-the-shelf' packages such as Click Funnels and Kartra offer.

So, if you're looking for a membership site that's even more sophisticated, you will need a web developer to help you create it, unless you have the skill sets yourself. I highly recommend Wildfire Information Systems (our web developer). Ian Entwistle, the managing director, runs a superb business and will build pretty much anything you need cost effectively (irrespective of the country you reside in). You can contact Ian via their website here...

www.wildfireinfosys.com

The membership site we have developed for our clients is called the Core Asset Vault. You can see a couple of screenshots from it shown as figures 3.10 and 3.11...

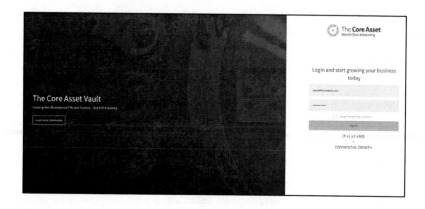

Figure 3.10: Login page for the Core Asset Vault

Figure 3.11: Dashboard for the Core Asset Vault

As you can see, it's highly professional and helps guide the client through our System (The FORMULA).

After each meeting, our business mentors simply direct the client to the right section of the Vault, and then the client has everything at their fingertips when they're ready to create and implement the tactic or strategy.

Hopefully, you can see why having an implementation system for the client, when combined with a mentoring system for you, really does make a huge difference to the success of your clients, and therefore to your success, too?

This really was a big part of the puzzle for me!

If you asked me what's made the biggest difference in terms of being a highly successful business mentor, I'd say everything I'm revealing to you when put together is, of course, significant, but the single biggest contributor has been developing and providing the implementation system for the client.

And, as I explained earlier, you don't have to start with an all-singing-and-dancing membership site. Start with your 'How To' guides, and build from there.

Even this will make a huge difference to your own success, because your clients will be able to competently apply the tactics and strategies you're advising them to implement without wasting joint time with constant toing and froing between you both.

Don't take this lightly.

Remember, your mentoring system is for you to guide your clients so you never have to 'wing it' with them.

It also keeps you both on track towards achieving the desired outcome your expertise is focussed on.

And the implementation system for clients is to ensure they can implement your advice to a high or at least competent level. BOTH are key tools of a world-class business mentor and combined together will ensure tremendous results for your clients (and you)...

Welcome to the start of *world-class* business mentoring!

What you need to do now is create a mentoring package that is irresistible to your potential clients.

That's what we'll focus on in the next chapter.

Chapter Summary

- The entire focus of your mentoring business must be on producing predictable and consistent results for your clients!

- Get this right, and you'll lay the foundation that will guarantee your success.

- To ensure clients get results you need two systems:

  - a *'Business Mentoring System'* for you to deliver your mentoring service to your clients in a systemised, structured and professional way;

  - and an *'Implementation System'* for your clients so they can apply the tactics and strategies you relay with them, quickly, easily and to a high level of competence.

CHAPTER 4:

MENTORING ATTRACTION PACKAGE (M.A.P.)

$$R \times \underline{M} \times L \times A \times M$$

When I was contemplating leaving Nottingham Rugby Club to join Leicester Tigers it was an agonising decision. At the time, Nottingham were better than Leicester. We were led by Brain Moore, the England and British Lions hooker ('Pitbull' to his friends!). He was an astonishing leader. In the second row was Chris Gray, voted best player for Scotland's tour of New Zealand in 1990. Gary Rees, another England player, was on the flank, and Simon Hodgkinson (back then England's record Five Nations kicker) played at full back. The rest of the team were accomplished players with several of us in England's 'A' team. The head coach was Alan Davies, who, as I mentioned earlier, would go on to coach Wales. We finished second in the league and only lost in the semi-final of the Cup with the last kick of the game.

Other than the semi-final defeat, when I was injured, I played in every game!

On the other hand, the Tigers finished sixth in the league and lost in the early rounds of the Cup.

I was already in the England setup. I'd played for the famed Barbarians several times, too, was regarded as one of the top wingers in the country behind England's record try scorer, Rory Underwood, his brother Tony and new England cap, Barry Evans.

The problem was... Rory, Tony and Barry were all at Leicester Tigers!

So, why on earth was I even contemplating leaving Nottingham to join an inferior team and risk not even getting picked?

It all came down to one thing...

...the 'OFFER'!

Tony Russ, the Leicester Tigers head coach, had approached me in the summer and put forward a compelling offer. Remember, back then rugby union was an amateur sport, so there were no money incentives (unfortunately!).

This is what he said...

"Steve, you're assured of your place at Nottingham, week in, week out. I can't promise you a starting place, obviously, but Tony is joining Cambridge University and isn't allowed to play for us until January after the Varsity (this is the annual match played between Oxford and Cambridge Universities at Twickenham, the home of England rugby). Rory needs to be rested for several matches before the Five Nations (back then the '5 Nations' was the Northern Hemisphere's top international rugby competition. It's now the Six Nations) and Barry isn't in my plans.

"Plus, instead of playing in front of 4,000 people at Nottingham, you'll be playing in front of 15,000 people... you'll be part of the biggest club in the world, and I'm building a team to win the league... and I want you to be part of it. Dean Richards (a legend of the game) is captain next year and has asked me personally to see if you'll join the Club (I had played with 'Deano' for the 'Midlands' against Australia in 1988. The match was at Leicester Tigers. We would lose 25–18, but I experienced firsthand what it would be like to play at the Tigers' Welford Road ground with Deano as captain. It was exhilarating, and Deano was an inspirational, uncompromising captain in the same mould as Brian Moore.

"I'm also speaking with the likes of Darren Garforth (who would go on to have a great England and Tigers career), Richard Cockerill ('Cockers' would also go on to have a successful England and Tigers career)... oh, and there's a chap called Martin Johnson, who I can tell you will become a legend of the game (how right Tony was: 'Johnno' would lead England to win the World Cup in 2003).

"We're also building what will be the finest training facility in the country, and it will be ready shortly after you join (if you join). Plus, I've assembled what I believe to be the best and largest back-room player support team in Europe (dieticians, speed and agility coaches – Merv Wilson, and first-team coaches Ian 'Dosser' Smith and Paul Dodge (both were Tigers legends, and I'd also played with both of them for the Midlands, so I knew them well). I'm putting all this in place to ensure you and all my other players become better rugby players, and I don't believe you'll get this level of training and support anywhere else. We're years ahead of everyone else. I'm basically putting the steps in place to create a professional, world-class structure which will be unmatched anywhere else!".

What Tony was doing was creating an irresistible package, albeit non-financial, but he really stacked each element of the 'offer' one on top of the other.

He made it virtually impossible for me to say NO... it was too compelling.

And it worked!

I joined the club in the summer, ready to fight for my place (I ended up playing 170 games, scoring 86 tries, so it worked out pretty well!).

So, what's the relevance of this story?

Well, that was my first exposure to someone creating a truly irresistible package, built progressively, benefit by benefit, to make it a 'no-brainer' for me to take action.

Also, notice that Tony had created all of this whilst being unable to offer me *any* financial incentive (well, I did get expenses at eight pence a mile – yes, the Tigers were generous back then)!

This experience taught me a vital lesson.

If you build an offer by adding more and more relevant and impactful elements on top of each other, as Tony had done, then it will become irresistible, and you make it a no-brainer for people.

Obviously, I didn't use the concept immediately, because it would be some five years before I would start Hackney Marketing. But what Tony showed me that day really hit home... and I would never forget the power of an *irresistible offer*.

So, when I eventually set up Hackney Marketing, the concept of the irresistible offer was etched permanently on my brain, and I did start creating attractive offers so business owners would happily invest!

But, as you will recall, because I'd set everything up originally with me at the centre of the business, rather than getting results for the client being pivotal to the business, the reality was that I couldn't really create a compelling offer. And it explains why things were tough for me until I started focussing on getting results for clients.

That's a 180-degree shift and dramatically changes everything when it comes to business mentoring and the irresistible package you can create for the client.

...and it explains why it's the very first thing you need to get right.

The concept of creating an irresistible offer is very powerful. I call it the 'Mentoring Attraction Package' ('M.A.P.').

In simple terms, your M.A.P. explains at a high-level what the client gets when they work with you as a mentoring client.

Just as Tony had done with me all those years before, you need to do the same thing and layer each element of your offer one by one on top of each other to make it a no-brainer for your prospective clients.

If you don't do this, I promise you that growing your mentoring business will be hard. You'll find it a real challenge to acquire mentoring clients and charge the right level of fees (at least four hundred pounds, dollars or euros per hour) and, worse, you'll struggle to retain them for a decent length of time.

But, when you get it right, it will be so much easier to grow your business, acquire a constant stream of mentoring clients, and charge fees that amaze your competitors.

Your M.A.P., when created correctly, will make your fee seem insignificant to the client. It will excite them. It will completely overcome any price objections you get, and it will make you magnetic to business owners looking for your skills and expertise.

So, how do you build and create your own powerful M.A.P.?

There are six key steps...

How to Build Your M.A.P. (Mentoring Attraction Package)

STEP #1: Identify Your Target Market

First of all, you must identify the type of businesses or business owners you're going to target. This is absolutely pivotal to the success and growth of your mentoring business. Most people don't give this enough consideration.

Your target market is simply the people and businesses you're going to specifically target for your mentoring services.

Even if your mentoring service can be applied to every business on the planet, you need to identify the types of businesses that are best suited to it and can, of course, afford to pay you handsomely for your services.

As an example, most of our business mentors target small businesses. We have a programme that is affordable for small businesses and, as I mentioned earlier, at the same time earns our mentors at least four hundred pounds, dollars or euros per hour.

We also have mentors who target small or medium-sized businesses in certain sectors, such as Event Management, Accountancy, Health and Fitness, Well-Being, IT and so on. I can't emphasise enough just how important this first step is for you.

Remember, you cannot be 'all things to all people'. You must never try and target everybody, otherwise you'll target no one.

I've got a really simple example that will explain exactly how to do this and why identifying the target market is such a powerful tactic...

We bought the house we currently live in in 2005. At the time, our children were 9, 5 and 3. Our previous house had a small garden (just what I wanted – low maintenance), but we wanted the children to have a large garden to play in, and that was at the top of our wish list. Helen found the perfect house with just under an acre of land – perfect for the children to play and roam around in safely.

But, of course, it came with a headache... maintenance and keeping the lawn and paddock neat and tidy.

I had no desire (and still don't) to do it myself, so one of the first things I did was to look for a gardener to come in each week to cut and trim the lawn and paddock.

Back then, the Yellow Pages was still in print, so I took out my trusty volume and looked under the category of 'Garden and Grounds Maintenance'.

Two ads stood out. Here they are shown as figure 4.1...

They both mention large or big grounds, but the top ad is so much more powerful and magnetic to its target market (people with large grounds or lawns).

Why?

Because it says 'Specialists in the Maintenance of Larger Domestic and Commercial Grounds'.

I didn't even bother ringing the people in the bottom ad (that's what happens when you get this right – it wipes out the competition once you identify your target market).

I spoke to Garden Care, and all these years later, they still maintain my grounds.

They could have tried a 'catch all' approach like Garden Busters are doing, but they don't. They just focus on people with large grounds... and saying they're 'specialists' in this area magnetically attracts their target market to them. It's not a great ad, but they have been successful because they identified their best market and make it clear that's their area of expertise (which, of course, it is).

It's NO different with your mentoring business. You need to identify your target market and call it out in your marketing.

As with all the tactics and strategies we use, I've broken them down into simple formulas you can use to make it easier for people to apply them.

Here's the Success Formula for creating a target market...

$$(I + A + T) = TM$$

Let's take a look at each part...

(I) IDENTIFY

Not all customers are created equal, and your mentoring business will naturally attract different segments of the market. So, the first part of the Success Formula is to identify those types of customers who are most likely to buy from you.

As I mentioned earlier, no matter what you think, you can't be 'all things to all people'.

Ask yourself the following questions to identify the best types of clients for your business...

- If relevant, what type of clients are buying from you already?

  Who are you naturally acquiring as clients? Look for similarities to help you create groups of people or businesses. These are most likely to be good targets for you.

- Who are your top clients?

  Find out who your best clients are. Look at your existing records. Look at their purchasing behaviour over the last 12 months.

- Can you easily reach these types of clients?

  If your marketing can easily reach these types of clients, (it's getting easier and easier, especially with the likes of

YouTube, Facebook, LinkedIn, Google Ads, Twitter, WhatsApp, Instagram and, of course, traditional methods such as email and that good old 'work horse'... direct mail). Write down the best methods to reach them. This will make it easy for you when you choose your lead generation marketing strategies later.

(A) AVATAR

Once you've identified your client segments, you need to build a simple profile of them (the Avatar).

You need to identify their commonalities such as...

- BUSINESSES – if your mentoring service/expertise fits in 'Category 1 or 2' mentioned earlier:

    Demographics (the average or typical characteristics of your target market): size, number of employees, age of business, turnover, location, number of directors, industry type, etc.

    Psychographics (what motivates the decision-makers in the business to take action – personal and business specific): behaviours, values, hobbies, impact of decision for the business and for them personally (will be different for each person involved in the decision-making process).

    Pain Points (what they need and want most): efficiency, ease of use, time, etc.

Common Objections (their most common reasons or buyer hurdles for NOT doing business with you): for example, cost, time, etc.

- INDIVIDUALS – if your mentoring service/expertise fits in 'Category 3' mentioned earlier:

  Demographics (the average or typical characteristics of your target market): age, annual income, education level, marital status, number of children, type of business they run, location, etc.

  Psychographics (what motivates them to take action): behaviours, values, hobbies, etc.

  Pain Points (what they need and want most): efficiency, ease of use, time, etc.

  Common Objections (their most common reasons or buyer hurdles for NOT doing business with you): for example, cost, time, etc.

Having done that, simply write down all those common characteristics on a sheet of paper. List them, one by one.

For example, here's the Avatar we created when targeting accountants for one of our mentoring programmes...

Accountant Member Avatar

Industry: Accountancy/CPA (not bookkeepers).

Business Type: Owner managed, single site, NOT home office.

Business Size: Sole practitioner and up to four partners maximum.

Psychographics: Looking to grow practice. Entrepreneurial. Willing to work to achieve results. Tried many other alternatives already. Frustrated. Sceptical. Good accountant.

Problems: Need to get more clients. Need to increase recurring fee income. Need to maximise value from existing clients. Find it hard to convert leads into new clients at the right fee. Pressured by low-priced competition and commodity selling. Frightened of big four taking a slice of the action. Worried about the impact of online accounting systems such as Xero.

Location: UK and Ireland, USA, Canada, Australia, New Zealand, South Africa.

Where Do They Hang Out: LinkedIn, Google, at their office.

Notice how defined the target market is. Once we'd nailed the Avatar, it was easy to then target those accountants, tailor our marketing to them and speak their language (focus on the psychographics).

The results speak for themselves...

Over a six-year period we acquired over 1,500 accountants into our mentoring programme!

(T) TAILOR

Once you know WHO you're targeting, you can then tailor your sales and marketing strategies to the Avatar. This is when you 'connect' with the potential client on a completely different level, and when they say or think 'this is for ME' (just like I did with the Garden Care ad earlier), your sales and profits will multiply!

This is where the psychographics really come into play, but you'll use your entire Avatar to ensure your marketing hits them right between their eyes, so to speak.

The reason is simple: if people see your marketing and immediately think 'this is specifically aimed at people like me', then your response rates will immediately increase.

I'll explain later how you then use all this information to create highly effective marketing that appeals directly to your chosen target market.

STEP #2: Set the Foundation

The next step – the M.A.P.'s foundation, if you like – is that it has to be focussed on one goal... to achieve RESULTS for your clients (your target market). As I've already said, this underpins everything you should do. That's why getting results for clients is the first part of the mentoring success equation.

Think about it... if your M.A.P. is focussed on delivering results for the client, then it will automatically be more irresistible to your prospective clients. All they want is results. They don't even really want a business mentor. They just want the results you will bring them. So, with this complete focus on results, your M.A.P. will stand out and draw your prospective client to you.

When Tony told me he was building a team to take on the best in the UK and Europe he was setting the foundation based on RESULTS. When he told me he had assembled the best and largest team of coaches and performance experts, as well as building the finest training facility in the land, he was setting the foundation for RESULTS!

STEP #3: Name Your Mentoring Service

Next, you need to name your mentoring service. This is part of the process of making your services tangible.

It may have escaped you so far, but what we're doing as we go through this whole process of building a successful mentoring business is taking an intangible 'service' and making it 'feel' more like a 'product'. If something is seen as intangible, it's much harder to sell. Something that's tangible, a product, is so much easier to sell, because it has features... you can see it, touch it, smell it and so on. Therefore, what you need to do is make your mentoring service as tangible as possible. It's one of the key outcomes of creating your M.A.P.

I learned this tactic many years ago after meeting a potential client. This was prior to me creating my first system. The prospect was a very successful lawyer. He had built one of the UK's most successful firms of lawyers with offices all over the country. He had been drawn to me from an ad I'd placed in a very large publication called the 'Solicitors Gazette' here in the UK.

I took him through my proposal for working with him and his firm, and he turned around to me and said (although I can't recall the exact words) something like, "Steve, thanks for coming to see me today. I like what you're doing, but I can't really see what it is you're selling. You're selling a service which, by its nature, is hard for people to appreciate what it can do for them. One of the reasons why we've been so successful is that we've made our legal services sound and feel like products. They all have specific names unique to us. They all have systems of delivery. They all have features and benefits. You're trying to sell me the result, which is what I want, but I can't see how you're going to achieve that."

Needless to say, I didn't acquire them as clients, but that meeting was the catalyst to immediately make my services more tangible.

So, naming your mentoring service is one of the things you'll do to make it more tangible. It's a simple tactic but highly effective.

For example, our mentoring service is called the Sales Accelerator Programme.

It's clear what the programme will achieve for the target market, and that's important. Don't try to be clever with the name of your service. Just give it a name that promises the end result your target market is seeking from your help.

STEP #4: Identify the Value Elements

After naming your mentoring service, you need to build the value in your M.A.P. You do this like Tony did with me by accumulating a set of highly desirable elements that the target market will find irresistible.

Simply write them all down and articulate each one in one (ideally) or two sentences.

Remember, when you add all these elements together, it needs to demonstrate incredible value for money.

But before you start, there are a couple of very important things I need to mention here...

First, the number and quality of your value elements will ultimately determine how desirable your mentoring service is to the target market and what you can realistically charge for it.

At the same time, it's a balancing act, because you need to add value elements that don't consume too much of your time.

Your ultimate goal should obviously be to ensure results for your client but, at the same time, to do so in the most efficient way.

The one thing you can't expand is your time. Unfortunately, there will only ever be 24 hours in a day. You can't work for all those hours. As a minimum requirement you need sleep each day. Most people need seven hours sleep a day to be highly effective. So that leaves 17 hours, not including time to eat, etc. Anyway, you get my drift. You need to be ruthless with your time management.

As I said, it's a fine balance... you MUST ensure the time you dedicate to each client will ensure their success, but it must not be to the detriment of the amount of time you need to dedicate. This is where your mentoring system and client implementation system help significantly.

Believe me, this really is very important. If you can create a mentoring system that allows you the time to work with many clients rather than a small handful, your earning potential will skyrocket. We'll talk later about putting in place a 'one-to-many' mentoring programme. In the meantime, the more you value your time and protect it, the more time you'll have to decide how you want to split it up and, if you want, to work with more clients.

What you now need to do is to write down the value elements you want to include as part of your mentoring service.

To give you an idea of what to include, let me take you through the value elements we include as part of the Sales Accelerator Programme and explain why they're so important...

- **24/7 Access to the Core Asset Vault**

  If you recall, the Core Asset Vault is our client implementation system. Including this as one of our value elements is, of course, very important. Remember, you're in the top 1% of mentors and coaches by having an implementation system for clients. It makes you stand out and has considerable value to the client.

- **Full Access to the Sales Accelerator Fill-in-the-Blank Templates**

If you can create templates as part of your implementation system for clients, they are an excellent value element.

- **Personal and Experienced Business Growth MENTOR**

Obviously, the business mentor would be YOU. This is THE most important value element.

- **Monthly Marketing Makeover**

Even though your clients will be creating the tactics and strategies based on your implementation system (How To Guides, etc.), there's always the risk that they still won't do a good job. But there is a great solution you can provide that adds value to your mentoring service, and it still won't eat into your time too much. I discovered several years ago that by including one critique per month not only adds considerable value to your overall proposition but also ensures the tactics and strategies created by your clients can be reviewed by the expert (you) quickly and easily. This is an example of what our mentors provide: a monthly 'makeover' of a piece of the client's marketing.

This is definitely one of the value elements that will take you additional time, so build it into your overall package. For example, our marketing makeovers take 10–15 minutes to complete.

I've found the best way to deliver a critique that has meaning to the client and enables them to quickly and easily improve what they've done minimise your time completing it is for you to create a 'scoring system' for your tactics and strategies.

I've found over the years that every tactic and strategy CAN be broken down into multiple elements, and then each of those elements can be scored in terms of how good they are.

Let me explain what I mean...

Our mentoring service is, of course, based around business growth, so the tactics and strategies we advise the client to implement relate to the growth of their business.

It's taken me a number of years to get this right, but I've discovered through thousands of tests that every type of marketing and advertising strategy CAN be broken down into nine elements. We call them 'Core Elements'.

Figure 4.2 illustrates how we show the Core Elements as part of our Marketing Makeover. As you can see, we display them like a 'Periodic Table', and we evaluate every marketing and advertising piece around these nine Core Elements. Each Core Element has a score range depending on its importance, but to keep it simple, let's say all 9 Core Elements can score from zero to ten. Zero means the client hasn't included it; 10 means it's the best it can be (it's rare anything scores a perfect '10'). So, the total possible score is 90.

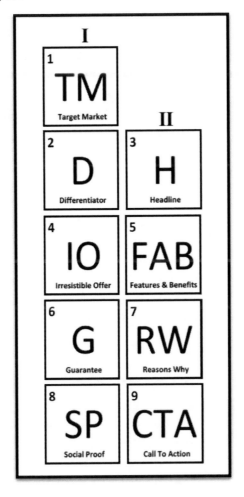

Figure 4.2: The 9 Core Elements
(the basis of our Marketing Makeover)

We first look to see if the Core Element is present in the tactic or strategy.

Then we take each Core Element in turn and score it based on our expertise. Obviously, this is a subjective evaluation, but that's where your expertise comes it. You know what *bad* looks like. You know what *good* looks like. And you know what *average* looks like. You'll be surprised how easy this is for you to do, and it shouldn't take more than 15 minutes to complete each critique once you've created your scoring sheet.

You may be surprised that any marketing and advertising tactic and strategy (web page, email, sales letter, leaflet, print ad, and so on) can be broken down like this, but it really is possible. And you can break down your own tactics and strategies like this.

Start with your 'How To' guides for each tactic and strategy. It's highly likely that most of the 'steps' are an important component part of that particular tactic or strategy and the basis for creating your scoring sheet.

What's important for you to understand is that a critique is *NOT* you reworking the tactic or strategy for the client. This is a BIG mistake many mentors and coaches make, because the moment you do that, you've gone from 'mentoring' and crossed the line into 'consulting' (and this should be paid work).

What you should do is simply provide the feedback via your scoring sheet, and the client will see where they need to make improvements based on your scoring of each part of the tactic or strategy. For example, if a client gets a critique back from me and, let's say, they score '2' for their 'Headline', then they know that they need to improve it. They then go back to the 'How To' guide on Headlines and make the appropriate adjustments.

You should also set a minimum total score requirement for each tactic and strategy. We tell clients that their target is to aim for a score of over 70 out of 90.

A word of caution here. Don't set your 'acceptable' score too high. Remember, clients don't have your level of skill or expertise, and you don't want to damage their motivation. So, don't be driven by perfection... that's simply not attainable.

'Good' is 'good enough'.

Hopefully, you can see the value in having a critiquing service. It will take time for you to build but, once in place, you'll love it and, once again, it will set you apart from every other mentor and coach!

- **Personal Support Pack**

  This is another great way to add considerable value without it taking up your time for every client.

  I deliver a webinar every month for all our clients. This is, of course, a 'one-to-many' approach, and it's easy to implement.

  You can easily run one for your clients every month, too, where you *invite them **all** to attend at the **same time***. To illustrate, you can, for example, cover a particular tactic or strategy, or interview clients on the results they've had working with you (case studies like this are always popular), or you can interview another expert.

  It doesn't have to be more complicated than that.

  We use WebinarJam to facilitate the webinars, but, as I mentioned earlier, there are a number of excellent webinar solutions available to you, such as GoTo Meeting and Zoom.

  Running a monthly webinar like this does require preparation, but even if it takes you a day to prepare and deliver, it's still only one day... no matter how many clients you have!

  Other things you can include as part of your 'support pack' include a monthly newsletter, additional training courses that you've created to help them, email support, monthly podcasts and so on.

What you simply need to think about is adding support elements that create value but don't eat into your time too much either.

As you can see, adding value elements to your M.A.P. isn't difficult, and they will all make your overall proposition highly desirable to your prospective clients. They will also help to retain your clients for longer (I'll cover this later).

STEP #5: Attach a Realistic 'Value Amount' to Each Element

Once you've added your value elements, simply give each one a sensible and realistic value amount. This is how you make your M.A.P. ooze value and demonstrate incredible value for money for the client when they sign up to your mentoring service.

I try to assemble my value elements so the total value of each element adds up to 8–10 times the actual monthly fee.

As you can see from figure 4.3, the five value elements of the Sales Accelerator Programme add up to £3,682, which is over nine times the £397 monthly fee.

If you create your value elements and, having set the value for each one, they don't total at least eight times your monthly fee, you need to think of one or two more value elements and add them to your list.

The Sales Accelerator Programme
What You're Going To Get...

- 24/7 Access To The Core Asset Vault (£797 Value)
- Full Access To ALL The Sales Accelerator Fill-In-The-Blank Templates (£397 Value)
- Personal & Experienced Business Growth MENTOR (£397 Value)
- Marketing Makeover (£797 Value)
- My Personal Support Package: ACCELERATE Webinar + Training Course (£1,294 Value)

Total Value: £3,682.00

 The Core Asset

Figure 4.3: The Value Elements and their corresponding value for the Sales Accelerator Programme

Don't just add extra value on to each of your value elements to reach the total – that doesn't work! Be honest with your value pricing and, if you have to, simply add more elements to your M.A.P.

I can't stress enough how important this is. Your M.A.P. is what your clients are buying. If it's not highly desirable and packed full of genuine added value, then it will be so much harder for you to acquire clients at the right fee.

Of course, follow my advice here: get your M.A.P. spot on and you're going to find it so much easier to acquire clients.

Chapter Summary

- Creating your own Mentoring Attraction Package (M.A.P.) is a critical part of your mentoring business. It will help you acquire as many clients as you want at the right fee!

- There are five steps to creating a powerful M.A.P...

  STEP #1: Identify Your Target Market
  STEP #2: Set the Foundation
  STEP #3: Name Your Mentoring Service
  STEP #4: Identify the Value Elements
  STEP #5: Attach a Realistic 'Value Amount' to Each Element

- The total amount of your Value Elements should be at least eight times the monthly fee you're charging for your mentoring service.

CHAPTER 5:

LEAD GENERATION

$$R \times M \times \underline{L} \times A \times M$$

One of my mentors emailed me the other day to say she was leaving our programme because (and I quote) "your system doesn't work. It's been six months, and I don't have a single client."

Ouch!

Is our mentoring system broke? Of course not. We have many mentors around the world who are very successful, primarily because they follow the advice in this book.

So, why doesn't it work for everyone?

I've got another sporting analogy to explain exactly why. It's a long story, but bear with me, because there are many lessons along the way...

As I mentioned at the start of this book, I was blessed with speed. I was also a good rugby player. During the mid-1990s I was recognised as one of the best wingers in the world.

My rugby journey started when I was 15 years old. Rugby wasn't my passion back then. I wanted to be a professional footballer, but by the time I'd turned 15, I'd realised I wasn't going to make it, and I wasn't enjoying it. I told Mum and Dad that I'd fallen out of love with football (which I had), and that I wasn't going to play again. They were shocked, and Dad said, "well what are you going to do now, son?"

I replied, "I'm going to play rugby".

The school I attended in the North East of England was primarily a football school (as most are in the North East), but one of the P.E. teachers, Martin Lyndley, was a part-time professional rugby *league* player but at school had played rugby union. He was a massive positive influence on me. He also played on the wing!

Because I was now dedicated to playing rugby, I, of course, improved quickly. Mr Lyndley would give me additional training practice at lunchtime and after school, and my learning back then was steep (thank you, Martin)!

England have a team at under-16 level, and they used to pick the team from a number of matches and trials based around the counties which divide the country. In the North there are six main counties: Durham, Yorkshire, Lancashire, Northumberland, Cumbria and Cheshire. I managed to get through the trials and was picked to play for Durham County Schools. If you got into the county team, you would then play a 'round robin' of matches against the opposition. North of England selectors would watch all the matches and select around 45 boys for a North of England trial... the first step towards playing for England under-16s.

I had a very good 'County Championship' and was selected for the North of England trials held in Cheshire at Macclesfield School.

I remember it being a horrendous day. It was snowing, and the wind was driving the snow across the pitch. Not my ideal conditions!

But I played an absolute storming match. I scored a couple of tries, one from my own 22-metre line (which means I ran over 80 metres to score, beating several opposition players along the way).

Everyone was congratulating me after the game and reassuring me that it was a formality that I'd make the team. I must admit I remember feeling that I'd done myself, my family and my school proud, and I had a knowing feeling that I'd done more than enough to make the North Of England team. I was very confident.

My position was number 14, and it was customary to read the team that had been selected from 15 down to one. In other words, my position was second to be read out. I remember they picked a lad called Mark Appelson (who would go on to be a really good player at Sale – a premiership club) at full back (15) and then my name was going to be next... but to my shock and dismay they named a guy called Martin Tomney at number 14 (I would later play with Martin at Loughborough University).

It turned out the selectors picked the entire Yorkshire back division for the North of England team. They all went to top private schools in Yorkshire such as Ampleforth, Sedbergh and Queen Elizabeth Grammar School (QEGS). It was my first taste of extreme bias in a team sport, especially a sport which had deep roots in private and public schools.

It was the first and last time I cried my eyes out after not being picked for a team and, as you can imagine, it really hurt.

But, did I blame the selectors? Did I blame the weather? Did I blame it on the fact that I had gone to a football-mad comprehensive school rather than a private or public school?

No, I didn't.

You know what I did?

I got busy.

I told myself I never wanted to feel like that again, and the only way to achieve that was to make it *impossible* for the selectors to *not* pick me.

So, I trained harder.

I worked harder.

At 16, I was training every day. I was even doing sprint training in winter on the path under the road lights just down from my house, and I would run home from my girlfriend's house, who lived just under three miles away, three times a week (as it happens my girlfriend back then when I was 16, Helen, is now my wife!).

Even though I was still only 16 years old, I had then moved on to the under-18 category. England also had an under-18 schoolboy team, and I vowed I'd do everything I could to make the team. The first match for England that season was to be against the New Zealand All Blacks (under-18 school team), who were touring the UK. Better still, the match would be played at Twickenham, the 'home' of English rugby.

To cut a long story short, I got picked to play in the match at Twickenham and, at 16 years and 5 months, I was the youngest on the pitch.

By sheer commitment and hard work, I'd overcome the bias of selecting players only from certain schools. I'd improved so much that I made it impossible for the selectors not to pick me. I was the only NON-public or private school boy in the England team that day.

Whilst I 'failed' to be selected at under-16 level, just 10 months later I was playing for England U18s!

But to achieve that goal took extreme effort. There was probably no other 16-year-old rugby-playing kid in the whole country training as hard as I was back then.

And if there's one thing I've learned since those days, it's that there will be setbacks. Things won't always go to plan. But, if you pick yourself up, dust yourself off and go again working even harder, then you are so much more likely to achieve success. I recently watched a speech by Denzel Washington, the great US actor, in which he said (and I quote), "If you fall down seven times, get up eight."

I wholeheartedly agree.

In my experience, far too many people give up too early and are only too happy to blame everyone else rather than themselves. Take responsibility for your life and the progress you make. Do NOT blame others for your situation. You have full control.

And that's the point I'm making here. The lady that was saying our system doesn't work, hardly put any effort into generating leads, yet she was more than happy to blame me and my team for her lack of application.

People with a blame attitude hardly ever make it in business and are far better off simply getting a job. But if you're prepared to work hard, apply yourself, learn, and take full responsibility for your success (or otherwise), then you're in for a real treat.

So, why talk about this now?

Well, your work ethic, of course, extends across everything you do, but, as obvious as it may seem, I can confirm that the success of your business (any business for that matter) is down to the amount of time and effort you put into building it and, especially, lead generation.

You can have the world's greatest mentoring service that achieves record results for clients, but if you don't generate leads, then you aren't going to get clients, and your service might as well be non-existent.

The lady I spoke about at the start of this chapter failed to apply the effort into her lead generation activity (even though we set everything up for her – see later), and there was only ever going to be one outcome as a consequence.

It's also important for you to remember that building any business is NOT easy. There isn't such a thing as a get-rich-quick business. There isn't such a thing as a magic bullet. However, as Tony Robbins says, "Success leaves clues." One of those clues is to work hard every day.

Are you with me still?

Great, so let's get back to lead generation.

Lead generation is simply getting your target market to, figuratively speaking, raise their hands and say, "Yes, I'm interested". Nothing more. Nothing less.

In my experience, this is the area in which most small-to-medium-sized businesses are weak, often very weak at achieving, yet, of course, it's vitally important. It's the reason why 80% of businesses go bust inside three years... they simply fail to sell enough of their products and services, and that can be attributed to their poor understanding of how to generate enough leads in the first place.

On the plus side, it's never been easier or better to generate leads. Back when I first started out, the internet was in its early stages of development, so to generate leads we had to rely on more 'traditional' tactics and strategies such as direct mail, telemarketing, print advertising, and radio and television advertising. The latter two were, of course, very expensive.

But now, the landscape has completely changed...

You've still got the traditional channels, as above, and you've also got everything online from email through to social media marketing and advertising on huge platforms such as Google, YouTube, Facebook, Twitter, Instagram and so on. Believe me, it's never been better or easier!

That said, because there's a proliferation of advertising and marketing platforms, it's become harder to choose the right channels. So, what I want to first do is explain what your options are and how you can approach generating leads.

To start with, I see most business mentors (and many other businesses) use just one main method to generate leads, and that's a dangerous and limiting approach. It's dangerous because if you use one tactic or strategy and for some reason it stops working, you've got a big problem on your hands. It's very important to use multiple lead generation strategies. Then, of course, you get multiplied results.

What you need to do is take a slightly different approach to the lead generation strategies you use. What I'm about to reveal is an approach that very few people outside our inner circle of mentors and clients use. I promise it is the best way for you to determine which lead generation strategies you should use for YOUR mentoring business. More importantly, it maximises your results, because you're not reliant on one tactic or strategy, or one main medium. In this context, when I talk about 'media', I am referring to the way in which your lead generation strategy is delivered to your target market.

Most people become reliant on one strategy and one medium. In fact, more often than not, they simply use the same media and strategies that all their competitors are using.

This could mean two things:

- In most cases the best medium isn't being used, and, as a result, neither are the best marketing tactics and strategies being used for the right target market(s).

- Existing marketing tactics and strategies are wasteful.

Furthermore, there can be a huge difference in results if you don't choose the correct medium.

It's been my experience that many business mentors (and most business owners in general) leave small fortunes on the table, simply because they have failed to **<u>choose</u>** the correct media.

The good news is that once you've defined the media, the lead generation tactics and strategies select themselves.

This is a very simple yet highly effective way to determine the right media channels to use for your mentoring business (we teach this to our clients, too).

First, let's look at the media channels available to you. As you can see, there are just three main media categories:

1. **E-Media**

2. **Published Media**

3. **Direct Marketing Media**

The table in figure 5.1 shows each media category and the associated strategies you can use for that particular group...

Media Category	Strategies
1. E-Media	• Website/Landing Pages • Webinar • Email Marketing • Google and Google Ads • YouTube Advertising • YouTube Channel • Facebook and Facebook Advertising • LinkedIn and LinkedIn Advertising • Twitter and Twitter Advertising • Other Social Media Platforms such as Instagram, Pinterest, etc. • Other Search Engines • Online Press Releases • ... etc.

Figure 5.1: Media Categories & Strategies

2. Published Media	• Classified Advertising • Newspaper, Magazine and Trade Press Advertising • Business Directory Advertising • Inserts • Radio Advertising • TV Advertising • Press Releases • ... etc.
3. Direct Marketing Media	• Seminars • Letters • Postcards • Flyers • Joint Ventures • Newsletters • Leaflets • Telemarketing • Networking • ... etc.

Figure 5.1: Media Categories & Strategies (continued)

So, how do you choose the right media channel category and combination of media channels for your business?

First, and this is important:

I recommend you use all three media categories to reach your target market(s). Tests have proved that if you use a combination of all three categories, your results massively improve.

Second, to choose the right strategies, all you need to do is ask yourself the following two simple questions:

1. Where can my target market be reached?

2. Where would the target market look to source our products or services?

The answers to these two questions will help you to determine which marketing strategies to use and are shown in figure 5.2...

CHOOSING THE RIGHT STRATEGIES		
Where can the target market be found?	**Media Category**	**STRATEGIES**
At work (or in the business)	Direct Marketing Media	• Seminars • Letters • Postcards • Flyers • Joint Ventures • Newsletters • Leaflets • Telemarketing

At home	Direct Marketing Media	• Seminars • Sales Letter • Postcards • Flyers • Joint Ventures • Newsletters • Leaflets • Telemarketing
Subscribing to trade press	Published Media	• Classifieds • Trade Press • Inserts • Press Releases
Internet	E-Media	• Website/Landing Pages • Webinar • Email Marketing • Google and Google Ads • YouTube Advertising • YouTube Channel • Facebook and Facebook Advertising

Internet (continued)	E-Media	• LinkedIn and LinkedIn Advertising
		• Twitter and Twitter Advertising
		• Other Social Media Platforms such as Instagram, Pinterest, etc.
		• Other Search Engines
		• Online Press Releases
Local newspaper	Published Media	• Classifieds
		• Newspaper
		• Inserts
		• Press Releases

Figure 5.2: Choosing the Right Strategies

As you can see from figure 5.2, you have numerous options in terms of the media category and then the strategies you should use. We'll get into the best tactics and strategies for your mentoring business shortly, but first I want to reinforce the one thing that more than any other will determine the success or failure of your lead generation: <u>being able to demonstrate your expertise</u>.

I call this concept *'Expertise FIRST'*.

Here's what it is and why it works so well...

Expertise First

I learned this concept while I was playing rugby for Leicester Tigers. It was just prior to me working with Tim Exeter, the speed and agility coach I mentioned previously.

Back in early 1997, a huge new industry was about to be born in world sport. It was called 'SAQ' – 'Speed, Agility and Quickness'. It was developed by Randy Smyth. Randy was a US 100-metre sprinter. He never quite made the US Olympic team, but he was fascinated by the human body and how it could be 'taught' to run faster and become more agile. Quietly, he had been developing a number of techniques and patented training aids and was working with a number of American football athletes, basketball players, baseball players and sprinters. His results were phenomenal.

He had taken the traditional speed and agility techniques that had been around for decades and built an entire range of products to shortcut the process of being able to run quicker and become more agile.

The problem he had was that no one, except his small group of athletes, had ever heard of SAQ or 'Speed City' (Randy's original company).

So, he decided he had to show people how it all worked (Expertise First).

He created the first-ever SAQ Super Conference. It was held in New Orleans in January 1997. Prior to the launch of the Super Conference, he had reached out to a number of agents across the English-speaking world that he had built relationships with over the years and asked them to source the fastest athletes in each country with a view to them becoming ambassadors for him and SAQ.

As I mentioned earlier, back in 1997 I was one of the fastest rugby players in the UK, and I received a call from Randy's UK agent (Alan Pearson), who had already been in touch with Leicester Tigers and, along with one of the Tigers' coaching team (former Australian second row Duncan Hall), I was given permission by the Club to be the UK ambassador for SAQ.

But before agreeing to do that, Randy invited us over to the Super Conference to see what the fuss was all about. During the three-day conference Randy took all these world-famous coaches and athletes in dozens of different sports across dozens of countries through all his techniques. He didn't ask anyone to pay a penny to attend.

In the back of his mind, he knew that once he showed the coaches and athletes the techniques, training aids and training programmes, he would instantly create the desire for his work and products. And boy was he right!

That single conference launched a new and radical training concept that revolutionised the speed and agility industry.

Actually, to be accurate, there wasn't even an industry before Randy. He created it.

And he created it using the concept I now call *Expertise First*.

Once Randy showed his expertise to his ideal target market (coaches and athletes), with their support he knew people would find it virtually impossible for them to NOT buy his products and programmes. And he was right.

Although most people aren't aware of this, Randy was the man who created the entire SAQ industry, and now his techniques and products are used by professional and amateur sports for all ages. If you have children and you see them running in between 'ladders' or jumping over small 'hurdles' and other speed and agility aids, the likelihood is they were all originally born out of Randy's Speed City.

Although I wouldn't use this concept for some years, Randy's SAQ conference made an indelible mark on me, especially the power of Expertise First. I can tell you that after that conference not one person had any doubts about Randy's expertise.... but, if he'd simply tried to sell his programmes and training aids first, rather than demonstrating his expertise, he would never have created such a successful international business, let alone within a three-day period!

One of the coaches who attended Randy's Super Conference was Tim Exeter, and that's why I ended up working with him, too!

You can apply this concept to EVERY business, but, of course, as a business mentor, Expertise First is an even more valuable and powerful concept.

To reinforce this, I can tell you I've tried numerous ways to generate clients... and Expertise First beats anything else by a landslide.

Ultimately, if you can demonstrate your expertise to your target market *prior* to selling your mentoring service, prospects are far more likely to become clients. In fact, I'd go as far as to say that if you get this right, you'll never, ever have to worry about where the next client will come from.

You can demonstrate this, as Randy did with his SAQ Super Conference, by giving away something 'motivating' **FREE**.

I call this an *'Expertise First Lead Magnet'*. So, Randy's Super Conference was his 'Expertise First Lead Magnet'. But you definitely don't need to go to the extremes or costs that Randy did.

Your Expertise First Lead Magnet can be something as simple as a one-page 'blueprint' of your service and why clients will get results (see figure 5.3 for an example).

Or, it could be a free demonstration of a part of your service or a special report or a piece of software or an app you create that guides the prospect through elements of your service (like our 'Sales Accelerator ROADMAP'). Or it could be a free critique (as discussed previously), or a book that you give away for free, or just for a small shipping and handling fee.

There really is no limit to what you can provide when it comes to Expertise First. Yes, it's quite a shift for most people... but I promise you... if you change your approach from selling...to Expertise First... you'll find it so much easier and more effective once you've created your Expertise First Lead Magnet(s).

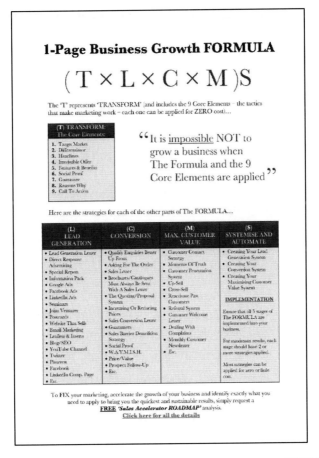

Figure 5.3: Example of a 'One-Page Blueprint' showing 'The FORMULA', our system for growing any business

To make things easier for you, here is some valuable feedback from my testing of numerous Expertise First Lead Magnets, and these are the top four and how to create them...

The Top Four Expertise First Lead Magnets

An effective Expertise First Lead Magnet is simply one that is highly desired by your target market. This must always be at the forefront of your mind when you're creating one. I've found that the top four Expertise First Lead Magnets, in no particular order, are...

1. Critique

2. Webinar

3. Software Diagnostic Solution

4. Monthly Printed Newsletter

Let's expand on each one in turn...

1. Critique

I explained about critiques earlier when describing your potential M.A.P. (Mentoring Attraction Package). The context, then, was providing one critique per month to your clients to build value in your mentoring service. But here's the thing: you can 'kill two birds with one stone' by using the same critique as an Expertise First Lead Magnet. A critique shows your expertise and provides valuable feedback for the potential client.

Now, one important point to mention here is DON'T ever email your critique to the prospect. It's vital you go through it with them, ideally via one of the online meeting platforms we discussed earlier. I'll explain shortly why that's so important.

Here's what you need to do...

STEP #1: Create Critique

I explained previously how to create your critique. Don't move to step 2 until your critique is ready.

STEP #2: Create Landing Page

You need a standalone web page for people to be able to request your critique. A standalone web page is also called a 'landing page' or 'squeeze page'. Other than your legal links (privacy, terms, disclaimer, etc.) there should be no other links on this page. Here's what you need to include on the page to ensure maximum conversion...

- <u>Headline:</u> Make sure that it's clear the critique is FREE and explain in less than 17 words what the critique will do for your prospect. For example...

Figure 5.4: Headline Example

- <u>Image:</u> Show an image of your critique to the left of your headline.

- <u>Explain How It Works:</u> Then explain how your critique works and how it will bring them the improvements you promise (you must link this to your results-producing system). See the example in figure 5.5...

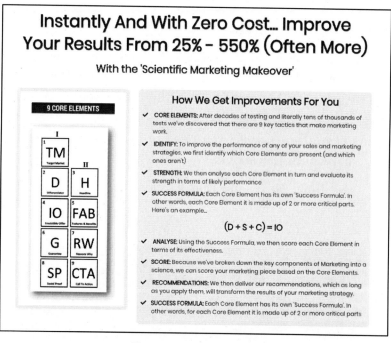

Figure 5.5: How It Works

- <u>Tell Them What/Where It Applies:</u> Then detail the area of the prospect's business where the critique can be applied (only relevant if there are multiple applications).

Include as many areas as you can. Every prospect is different, so the more scenarios you include, the better.

See the example in figure 5.6...

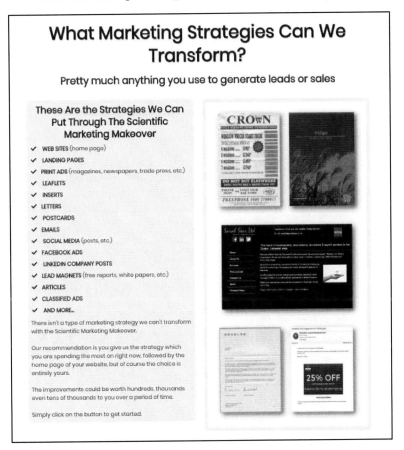

Figure 5.6: Where the Critique Can Be Applied

- <u>Explain the Steps:</u> Finally, simply go through the process that you'll be taking your prospect through, from the moment they click on the 'call-to-action button' (the 'button' prospects click on to take the next step) to you presenting the findings of the critique.

See the example in figure 5.7…

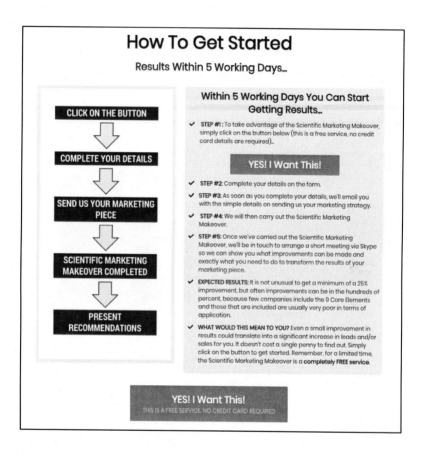

Figure 5.7: Explain the Steps

- <u>Call-to-Action Buttons:</u> Make sure you add 'buttons' on your landing page so the prospect can take the first step. When the button is clicked, it should open a simple form so the prospect can add their details.

- <u>Form:</u> Your form needs to be linked to your CRM (customer relationship management) system so you can record the details of everyone who requests your critique and then follow-up with them (see next). see example in figure 5.8...

Figure 5.8: The Form

- <u>Thank-You Page:</u> Once a prospect enters their details on the form and they click the button, they should be directed to a 'Thank-You Page'. This is a really important step. Here's why...

Firstly, your Thank-You Page will simply let them know that you have received their request for the critique. Secondly, and importantly, you should include a button on the page that takes the prospect directly to your *online diary*.

Yes... your ONLINE DIARY.

This is another world-class step. Putting this in place is very professional and, crucially, means your prospects are taking the positive step of booking their critique meeting... without you needing to go back and forth trying to arrange a suitable time. It will save you a mountain of time and makes this critical step really easy for the prospect.

It also means you don't have to lift a single finger in the entire process (once set up) until you actually meet with the prospect to deliver the critique.

There are many online diary applications to choose from. We use Timetrade (www.timetrade.com).

- <u>Follow-Up Campaign:</u> However you choose to carry out your critique, it's important you deliver the results <u>at the critique meeting</u>, which should be conducted via an online meeting platform. Your follow-up should include anything you need from the prospect so you can complete the critique professionally.

  You will also need a separate campaign to follow-up with those prospects who don't submit the required information (for obvious reasons, I call this a 'nag sequence').

2. Webinar

In simple terms, a webinar is an online seminar. You deliver your webinar using an online webinar platform such as

WebinarJam or GoTo Meeting, etc., and your delegates take part online in the comfort of their home or office.

I've been running webinars for over 11 years and, of course, the technology and the strategies have improved significantly since those early days.

There are two formats of webinar you can run: 'live' or 'pre-recorded'.

My advice is for you to first run your webinar as a live one and, once you're happy with it, you can then move onto a pre-recorded or what we call an 'evergreen' webinar. The latter is my favourite, because it can be fully automated (see below for more details).

The main advantage of running a webinar is that you use the webinar to demonstrate your expertise, and then you set it up so you acquire clients at the end of it... and in the days that follow.

In other words, it doubles up as an Expertise First Lead Magnet and your conversion system (see later) *all at once*.

I'll be brutally honest here and say it takes me around two full weeks to create a webinar. It's a huge piece of work, but, as long as you follow my advice, I can tell you that those two weeks of time and effort will pay you back many times over.

Plus, if I had to give you my top five Expertise First Lead Magnets, then fifth on the list would be a seminar. And the great news is that once you've developed your webinar, it can be used with minimal changes as your seminar, whereby you deliver the content in a 'live' environment to a room full of people!

Okay, so let's dive in! Here's what you need to do to create your webinar...

STEP #1: Write The Script

Creating the actual script you'll deliver during the webinar is the most important element and therefore the most time-consuming.

No matter how accomplished you are, I strongly urge you NOT to deliver the webinar without a script, especially the first few times you deliver it. Truthfully, I know results are impacted when I go 'off script', so I've never delivered any of my webinars without the discipline of using my script.

The good news is there is a simple process you can go through that will enable you to create a very powerful and engaging webinar that will lead to delegates joining your mentoring programme.

Here are the stages of building your webinar script. After each stage, I've added the exact script I use in our webinar to acquire clients for our mentors...

- STAGE #1: Create the Title of Your Webinar

  The title of your webinar is very important. This is what will grab the attention of your target market, and it plays a huge part in them either registering or not for your webinar.

  I've tested hundreds of different concepts, and, without question, the 'How To...' title is the best and safest approach.

What follows the 'How To...' should be the biggest benefit that your mentoring skills and expertise will bring to your delegates.

For example, my expertise is helping business owners grow their business, even if they have no sales and marketing expertise or huge marketing budget. So, this is how I would write the title of the webinar...

'How to Add an Additional 7-Figures to Your Business in the Next 12 Months Without Wasting Valuable Time, Spending a Fortune on Marketing, or Having to Become a Marketing Pro'

- STAGE #2: Welcome, Incentive to Stay Tuned Until the End, and Build Credibility

Obviously, at the start you should welcome and thank everyone for joining you on the webinar.

Then I advise you to give those who have attended an incentive to watch the webinar until the end. I learned this from Andy Jenkins at WebinarJam, and it's a great tactic. Your incentive can be anything that you believe will be desirable to your target market. For example, it could be your one-page blueprint of your results-producing system... just think of a special bonus that they can't get anywhere else (and so on). But, be careful... don't make it something that takes a long time to consume. You don't want to distract them.

Then you need to explain why you're 'qualified' to talk to them. This basically means you need to explain your expertise or, in other words, you have 'earned the right'. This means that, from the start, you've convinced delegates that they will learn valuable insights from you.

Example (and please bear in mind this is *conversational*. You want to immediately put everyone at ease, to *bring them in*. Most people do much better if they write their script in a conversational style. Remember, most of us 'switch off' when we receive a sermon!)...

Hello, everybody, I'm Steve Hackney, good afternoon, good morning, good evening, depending on where you're from.

Welcome to the webinar. We've got people registered from all over the world, so before we get started please say "hello" in the chat box and let me know where you're from...............

And, while we're waiting for everyone to join, I just want to say that I'm really excited to be sharing this webinar with you today.

People say to me: Steve, what do you like talking about most, and it's this... talking about the FORMULA and the amazing effect it can have on the people and businesses that apply it. I'm going to show you some really cool stuff today. I'm going to show you how you can apply the FORMULA and get results the very same day. You're going to love it. So... a couple of things before we get started. I'd recommend taking out a pad and paper. Take notes, shut down Skype, turn your phone off, turn your email off.

I don't want you to miss anything. This will be fun, but it will be more fun if you interact with me. Make sure you're asking questions in the chat box, so I get feedback and can give you exactly what you want. And stay tuned until the end of the webinar, because, as I promised, I'll give you the link to download the FORMULA so you can easily apply it to your business, too. Okay, I'm ready to get started. Let me know you're ready...

Okay, 500 yes's right now.

Right... let's jump in...

Okay, the title of the webinar today is How to Add an Additional 7-Figures to Your Business in the Next 12 Months Without Wasting Valuable Time, Spending a Fortune on Marketing, or Having to Become a Marketing Pro". Are you guys excited about that? Okay, great. A couple of things before I get started...

First, I want to give you my earnings disclaimer. Obviously, after watching this webinar, a million isn't going to magically appear... you guys are smart enough to know that.

But, if you follow and apply what I'm giving you today... you WILL get positive results as soon as you do... then as you keep applying more and more of the formula, you'll REALLY begin to see major changes in your business.

That's what happens when you apply THE FORMULA. And I'm sure you'd like to create something that keeps growing and something that has longevity, well... that's exactly what THE FORMULA gives you. And today you're going to see a lot of actual PROOF: examples and case studies from people who are generating hundreds of thousands and millions a year all because of The Formula. Some of you will see big increases quickly, others it may take a bit longer. But even if it takes you 12 months to add hundreds of thousands to your business, I'm sure you'd be happy with that, right? In fact, just type *yes* into the box if that's the case...

Okay great... I thought so... brilliant.

The first thing I want to mention is that if you've failed at marketing or growing your business in the past, it's not your fault. There's a lot of information out there, and it can be confusing. In fact, information overload and bad advice is the reason why most business owners fail – it keeps you from succeeding. I come across it all the time, and it's okay, it's normal.

You see, marketing and advertising companies – no offence intended if we have any here today by the way guys!... they want you to think you need a lot of money and THEIR help in order to become successful. I'm here to tell you they're wrong.

And, by the way, some of your friends and family want you to fail, too! They don't benefit from your success. They like you just the way you are. They like to tell you 'that'll never work' or 'you're crazy for even trying it'. But I'm different! As a fellow entrepreneur, I'm part of an elite group, and we care deeply about our successes and truly want to see each other living the life of our dreams. Entrepreneurs like us thrive and get excited by the success of other entrepreneurs; it's what keeps us going, and if I know I've played a small part in helping others, then that's even more of a reason.

So, that's what we're here for today. I know you have a dream to build a successful or more successful business and make an impact, and I want to show you how to make that happen during this webinar.

My goal for this presentation is to help two types of people. For those who have new or relatively new businesses, you'll get a proven formula for growing your business that's easy to implement and gets your small or medium-sized business moving fast, so you never have to worry about money again. How many of you fit this profile?... (pause).

Okay, a few of you. Plus, for people who have a more established business, you'll also get the SAME formula, but I'll show you how to SCALE your business and ensure that you're also capitalising on all your assets – many of which are hidden assets already in your business – so it catapults your business forward at a rate of knots you've never seen before. Which of you already have an established business and would like to achieve all that? ... (pause).

Okay, great.

But before we get into it... let me tell you a little about myself. For the last twenty years or so, after my professional rugby career with Leicester Tigers and England came to end back in the mid-nineties, I've been helping small and medium-sized companies to increase their sales and grow their businesses.

In the early days it was really frustrating, though. You see, coming from an elite sporting background, everything was systemised, and providing you followed the system, you improved... but with businesses it wasn't that straightforward, as I'm sure you all know.

What I thought would intuitively work, didn't, and when one strategy would work brilliantly for one business it wouldn't for another. It was really frustrating until I discovered THE FORMULA, and when I did... it completely changed my life and the thousands of people we work with.

In fact, I just want to read a short passage from someone you may have heard of. His name is Sir Clive Woodward. For those of you who don't know who Sir Clive is, he was a very good rugby player, playing for Leicester, England and the British Lions, but he's better known for turning England's rugby union team from also-rans into world champions in 2003. He's known for pushing the boundaries in sport and business, and here's what he said...

"Winning. It's been at the heart of everything I've done since my early days at school, whether that's in sport or in business. My entire philosophy has been based on one simple formula: work hard, lay the right foundation and model and implement what the best are doing. Do that, and you'll outperform the competition.

This approach has served the people and teams I have been lucky enough to work with along the way, extremely well, not least the England rugby team. So why am I writing this about Steve Hackney?

There are two reasons.

Firstly, I've known Steve since he played for me back in my England days, and I've come to know what a successful person he was and is now. But the second is the most compelling reason, and that's because everything he does in a business context is about improving performance and winning. And this time it's about your performance and it's about you winning the marketing game for your team and for your business. For example, so many so-called gurus or experts don't go far enough. They stop short at telling you exactly what you need to do to win in the subject area that they cover, but they omit key details and leave you hanging.

Steve's different. You see, whether you like it or not, your success in the field of battle comes down to not just what you do, but how you do it. That's the game of success. And Steve has discovered exactly what it takes to grow any small or medium-sized business. He's found the success FORMULA. In my experience, when you combine multiple high-performance tactics as Steve has done here, that's when you start to see positive changes in whatever you're doing. I would go as far to say he's given you what I would call a success blueprint."

Okay, I hope that gives you a fair bit of confidence that I really do know what I'm talking about. But, as I said earlier, before THE FORMULA, results for my clients were inconsistent, so let's get back to how I discovered THE FORMULA and exactly what it is!

- ## STAGE #3: Explain 'Your Story'

People love stories, and you should weave as many relevant stories as you can into your script. One of the most important stories is how you became the expert you are. Don't fabricate it. Just tell everyone exactly how you developed your skills and expertise.

Example...

> I started Hackney Marketing in November 1995. At this point let me say, I was lucky. I didn't start my business under the normal stress and pressures many of you will have faced. I was at Leicester Tigers, back then the richest rugby club in the world, so I was earning a good living playing rugby.

> The business from day one didn't have to provide for me and my family, and the goal was simple... build it so when my rugby career ended, I would seamlessly transition from pro rugby player to business owner.

So, in my spare time, and there was a lot of it, because we only trained twice a day for a couple of hours... I studied everything about marketing and sales.

I even bought a speed-reading course which helped me get through over 1500 sales, marketing and personal development books in just 18 months. I created files on my computer, and anything that stood out as being really, really good that I could use in my own business and with clients; I created files for it. This completely 'tailored business growth library' became my sales and marketing tactics and strategies resource centre.

I then started to use them, first to build my business and get clients, and second to help my clients grow theirs. I then created detailed reports on all my results and the results of all my coaching and consulting clients.

And I quickly learned that most small and medium-sized businesses didn't have an end-to-end business growth system. There was nothing out there that said start here, and then, if you apply these steps and keep applying these steps, you're going to grow your business. Sure, there were people that were offering how-to products – you know, how to write advertisements, how to write Yellow Pages, and how to produce faxes that get results. Some of these things, as you know, are pretty much out of date now.

But nothing was around that was an end-to-end system for business owners to use. And that, if you like, was my opportunity. And I created something called the Power

Marketing System, which is a toolbox, as it says here, that literally went crazy.

We'd pack five big manuals, put them in a big box and send them all over the world. I mean, in the end we were working with customers in 46 different countries worldwide. This is a picture of the audio programme. Look, it's got cassettes! Some of you won't even know what cassettes are! (laugh)

But there was a problem. About half of the sales we made were returned because not everyone got results. Now, okay, some people just didn't do anything with it... so of course they were never going to get results. But I was really bothered about those who'd tried and it didn't work for them. To be frank, it was soul destroying.

And then I had a BREAKTHROUGH.... and from an unusual source! One day, my wife Helen could see my frustration. She asked... Stephen... (she calls me Stephen not Steve...) what's the matter? Normally, we NEVER talk business, but she could obviously see I wasn't happy about something. Helen, by the way, is a successful mathematician and studied maths at university, which, as you'll now see, is very important...

I told her I was really frustrated that my system didn't work for everyone. She asked me why I thought that was, and I said I believed that although it was a system, people would often hand-pick a few tactics and strategies, the ones they liked the sound of and just applied them. They may even apply more, but because it was ad hoc, they weren't putting a system in place, they were putting a mish mash of strategies in place, which means the building blocks and the solid foundation wasn't being applied and ultimately that would affect results. And, more importantly, it relied too heavily on the skills and expertise of the business owners in sales and marketing. Helen looked at me and then said... and I'll never forget it... it's obvious Stephen, you don't need a system for growth... you need a FORMULA.

I wasn't quite sure what she meant. She said: look, one thing I know as a mathematician is that a formula is a constant. It can't be broken. No matter how many millions of people apply it, and regardless of their skill or experience... they apply the formula and everyone gets the exact same result. A formula is solid. It's undeniable. For example, let's take the most simple of formulas, and that's the formula for calculating the area of a rectangle. It's simply $L \times W$ = the area of a rectangle, where L = length and W = width. You can't mess with that.

She was so right. It was a real 'eureka' moment for me. Sometimes you need someone else's perspective, and what she said was genius. You see, although systems are great, you need a structure to put them in. I didn't have that. I just had a set of tactics and strategies as part of a system, but I was missing the formula that would ensure no one could misinterpret exactly what to do, one that didn't rely on skill or expertise, and one that would guarantee the foundation for growth.

That moment literally transformed everything. And even now, although that happened some 15 years ago, I remember it like it was yesterday. Interestingly, it didn't take much time to create my first formula, because most of the components were already in the system. I just needed to organise things logically to ensure the foundation for growth was put in place.

In fact, this is an image showing it. As you can see, it was ugly and more complicated back then. And don't think, 'that doesn't look simple', because, as you're going to see, over the last decade or so, the formula has become super-simplified and more effective with each simplification... and I'll take you through it shortly. But, of course, creating a formula is one thing, but making sure it works and can't be broken is another. More importantly, it needed to work for EVERY type of small or medium-sized business. I needed my sample group and as big a group as possible.

We decided to create a programme for accountants in order to share the formula and our toolbox with their clients. So, 10 years or so ago, we started what became the largest sales and marketing network for accountants. At its peak, we had 1,500 accountants as members from all over the world, each with an average of 250 small and medium-sized business clients. That's a market or sample size, if you like, of 375,000 businesses.

We gave their clients the formula and access to our online toolbox of every successful sales and marketing tactic we'd ever proven, and with the help of the accountants... we documented results. It was arguably the largest test ever conducted into marketing and growing small and medium-sized businesses. It produced tens of thousands of results across hundreds of different industries. It also showed us the exact strategies within each component of THE FORMULA that were quick to apply, had a lasting effect and worked irrespective of the size of the business, irrespective of the industry and irrespective of the age of the business. So, are you guys, ready to see it?... (pause)

- ## STAGE #4: Show Them Your System and Add Social Proof

Next, give them a high-level view of your results-producing system. This is NOT your mentoring system. This is a high-level view of your client implementation system. For me, in my example, it's THE FORMULA.

Then, you need to start making this 'real' for your attendees. That means you need to start adding proof that you can deliver on your promises. In other words, you provide written or video testimonials from the people you've helped.

If you don't have any client testimonials, then I urge you to get them as soon as you can. Proof that you get results is absolutely key to you getting clients. So, even if you have to offer your services for free to three or four carefully selected people in return for a written or video testimonial, then do it. Please do NOT underestimate how important this is.

Video testimonials are, of course, the best source of social proof, but you can use written testimonials and screenshots of comments on social media (such as Facebook and LinkedIn). I use all three and weave them throughout the presentation.

Example...

> Okay great... here goes...
>
> Here it is... let me take you through it.
>
> This FORMULA is now PROVEN to grow ANY small and medium-sized business, irrespective of your skills or expertise. It's easy to implement, is currently being successfully used by over 26,000 businesses all over the world, and is responsible for adding hundreds of thousands even millions to each and every one of them.
>
> I'll repeat... no matter what business you're in or how new or established it is, THE FORMULA WILL apply to you. You see, here's how most people try and grow their businesses... they first tend to copy what the competition are doing or try and replicate what they did in their last job. They pick up some ideas from other businesses in different industries... they put up a website and then add other tactics and strategies and shiny, new buttons like social media, Google Ads and Facebook advertising, and whatever they read about or get sold to by marketing and advertising companies.
>
> But the problem is... it's all a bit haphazard. None of it follows a proven formula. None of it is based on a solid

foundation of what works. So, no matter what you add, without this foundation or the framework of THE FORMULA in place, it's highly unlikely to work or work as well as it should.

THE FORMULA makes growing your business predictable, because it focuses on the primary growth areas of your business... growth areas that EVERY business has. The FORMULA enables you to generate more leads, to convert more of your leads into clients, customers or patients, and to maximise the sales and profit from every single client, customer or patient you acquire. And that's ultimately how you grow a business, not by patching everything together adding sticky tape and hoping it's all going to hold together. Without foundations, it's impossible to get sustained results, and that's what THE FORMULA gives you... the foundation for growth, PLUS all of the proven tactics and strategies to build a highly successful business and do it quickly.

Just to explain what's possible, here's a story about Shafiq, who runs a normal general practice accounting firm. He'd not been growing the practice very quickly the past few years and was getting more and more frustrated with the ups and downs of sales and income and the amount of money he was able to take home. He tried all the usual avenues... He got an agency on board to build his social media... He advertised on Yell, which is a large online business directory in the UK... He redeveloped his website, which cost a few thousand pounds, but none of this worked as he'd hoped despite his throwing a lot of money at it, not to mention the time he'd spent on it. But when he came across THE FORMULA, he very quickly applied it, and his practice doubled in size within six months... and he did it at very little extra cost and without spending a lot of time on it either! Oh... and more importantly, Shafiq was and is a great accountant... but he is no sales and marketing genius! So, who else would like to double their business in the next 6–12 months or so? Or grow it by 50% or even 25%. Just write in the box what percentage you'd really like to grow your business by during the next 12 months... (pause)

- <u>STAGE #5: Your Three Big Secrets</u>

People always want to know the secrets to solving their problems. That's why I urge you to base the main part of your webinar on the three key secrets that your expertise will give your delegates.

Each secret should be based on the solution to your target market's most pressing challenges and misconceptions.

For example, if your expertise is based around getting the staff of a business to take ownership of their roles and drive the business forward without senior management having to get involved, then you need to think about what the business owners' biggest challenges are in this area and what their misconceptions are.

Here's how I'd tackle this to create your three big secrets...

First, my expertise enables businesses to create world-class teams and record profits. Common misconceptions could be (1) I need to micro-manage all my staff, otherwise they don't work hard (2) staff simply don't get motivated to achieve the goal of the business, and (3) non-sales staff are a cost rather than an asset to the business.

What we now need to do is turn each of these misconceptions into secrets...

SECRET #1: Getting your entire team to work in harmony to produce record-breaking profits.

SECRET #2: Take any under-performing team and transform it into a highly productive unit without you having to micro-manage them.

SECRET #3: Instantly turn each team member into a money-making asset, even if they're not in sales.

Do you see how that works? If you are a business owner with a fragmented bunch of people, and you're frustrated by having to keep them focussed every few minutes (that'd be many business owners!) then each *secret* would be highly appealing to you, right?

Example...

> Here's what we're going to cover in the next 45 minutes or so...
>
> Secret #1: Formula Duplication – "How to Get Instant Results by Duplicating Success (THE FORMULA) And Seamlessly Applying It To Your Business"

> Secret #2: Strategy Cloning – "How to Clone Each Growth Strategy Like a Seasoned Marketing Pro"

> Secret #3: Beat The Clock – "How to Then Successfully and Confidently Implement Each Expertly Created Strategy Often in 60 Minutes... or Less"

- ## STAGE #6: Take Them Through the Secrets

Now, simply go through each of the three secrets. Ideally, you should use a story to explain each one so they become as vivid as possible for your delegates. Also, weave in client testimonials to reinforce how powerful each secret is.

Example...

> Secret #2: Strategy Cloning – "How to Clone Each Growth Strategy Like a Seasoned Marketing Pro"

> Okay, the FORMULA and its magic is now firmly in place in your business, but that's just the framework. You've also transformed the results of your existing sales and marketing tactics and strategies. What you need to do now is add the proven tactics and strategies to each component of THE FORMULA, and it's this secret that's key to you accelerating your growth and adding six or seven figures to your business in the quickest time possible.

> And over the years, but especially after all the testing, we've currently created 38 proven strategies and tactics that any business can use to grow and increase profits.

They are all conveniently located in our 24/7 online resource called The Core Asset Vault. In fact, here's a screenshot showing The Core Asset layout after you log in. As you can see, it's structured to ensure THE FORMULA is automatically duplicated into your business, with the five components of THE FORMULA here. Behind each of these are the tactics and strategies that can be applied to each component of THE FORMULA.

As I said earlier, we have nine tactics and strategies that will transform your marketing. There are 14 lead generation tactics and strategies that will ensure you generate a constant stream of leads; 13 conversion tactics and strategies to ensure you convert a much higher percentage of leads into sales and new clients, customers or patients; 11 tactics and strategies that will maximise sales and profits from new and existing customers; and three systems that will help you put your growth and sales on autopilot.

That's a lot of proven strategies, and I bet you're thinking... "Wow!... that's going to be a real challenge to create dozens of strategies." And in normal circumstances you'd be right. Plus, you'd be constantly wondering if you're doing it right. I mean you only get to know what works by launching these things and testing, right?

Well it used to be the same for me, too.

When I was consulting, I used to create a brand new strategy for every single business. Each one literally took ages to produce.

Those of you who've tried to write a sales letter or web page, or an ad for your local newspaper or magazine, or even a simple one-page customer welcome letter, will know exactly what I mean... and bear in mind I know what I'm doing, but it still took hours, sometimes days, to create this stuff. Then one day when I was struggling for time, I just cloned a strategy that worked for a different client in a different industry, and to my amazement it worked. I mean it was equally successful. And by cloning, I simply took a strategy that had proven to work before with a client and then tailored the content to the other clients' business.

Just like copying what successful people do every day will help you achieve success; amazingly, it's the same with marketing and growth. It can be copied. Cloned. Replicated. And I've done it since thousands of times.

In fact, I remember listening to Tony Robbins a few years ago, and he said, "If you want to achieve success, all you need to do is find a way to model those who have already succeeded."

So, I started building up a huge portfolio of all the actual sales and marketing pieces that had worked well for me and my clients over the years. There are several hundred and the list is growing daily, and each is relevant for a particular strategy. Then I created step-by-step, fill-in-the-blank Sales Accelerator Templates, which keep the key components of the strategy but make it easy for anyone to clone it.

For example, we have Sales Accelerator Templates on how to transform your existing sales and marketing strategies, Sales Accelerator Templates on generating more leads, Sales Accelerator Templates on converting more leads into sales, Sales Accelerator Templates for maximising customer value, and Sales Accelerator Templates for systemising and automating those areas.

But to make it even easier, every single tactic and strategy has its own formula. I call it a 'success formula'. The success formula is kind of like a checklist. As long as you've got each element of the success formula in that particular tactic or strategy, your success is assured.

So, together, the fill-in the blank Sales Accelerator Templates and the corresponding success formulas are all you need to clone a tactic or strategy and ensure right out of the gate that you get results.

Let's just pause for a second and imagine you had to start this process from scratch. You now know the surprising truth that marketing success can be modelled... or cloned.

First, you have to find what works, then you can clone it. Obviously, you don't want to clone a strategy that doesn't work, so you have to be certain it's already successful. And you need to do that for every tactic or strategy. That's how you shortcut your path to growth and increased profit. And hopefully, that's exciting for you, just like it was for me. You can do it, but of course it will take some time before you build your own portfolio of proven strategies that can be cloned.

For example, Gary Pierce runs a couple of children's nurseries on the Isle of Man, a small island in the Irish Sea between the west coast of England and Ireland. It has a population of just 83,000. Surprisingly, Gary has a number of competitors, even though the island is relatively small. He has no sales and marketing expertise, but this is what he did...

He first duplicated the formula, applying it to his business, and then one of the first things he focussed on was the maximising-customer-value part of the formula, because like almost every small and medium-sized business, he wasn't tapping into this rich vein of income and profit. So, he took one of the 18 referral systems we've developed, cloned the fill-in-the-blank Sales Accelerator Template for it, made sure all elements of the success formula were present, and then launched it.

Here's what happened. In fact, this is a comment from Gary himself...

"We created a referral programme using the Referral System templates and examples in The Core Asset. We spent just £2,300, and in the first three months it generated £154,000 in extra sales."

Now that was just in the first three months. He's since systemised and automated this referral system, and it keeps generating this level of income every quarter. You see, modelling success is easy if you have the tools and the already proven tactics and strategies. The fill-in-the-blanks Sales Accelerator Templates and success formulas make it a cinch for you to clone any or all of the strategies to your business, no matter how little sales and marketing experience you have.

Think about it. Even if you launched a referral strategy and it produced only a tenth of what Gary's doing, I'm sure an extra £60,000 profit a year from just this single strategy would be welcomed. In fact, just let me know if this would be worth having in your business. Just type *yes* into the box... okay, great. So, are you starting to see what's possible?

As an aside, notice I said Gary had a number of competitors on the island.

Well, if you're also in a very competitive market, and to be frank, who isn't?... Then THE FORMULA will make it even easier to get clients, customers or patients and help you magnetically attract them from your competitors, just like Gary has done. Seriously, your competition will wonder what's hit them, as soon as you apply THE FORMULA and the tactics and strategies in The Core Asset.

Here's another quick story about how easy it is to clone the tactics and strategies. Remember, just to make sure you fully appreciate it... because of the Sales Accelerator Templates and success formulas you don't need any experience in sales and marketing. In fact, you can pass on the creation and cloning of the strategies to anyone in your team. If you've got a 14-year-old son or daughter, they can do it, too.

Well, Michael Thickpenny was no different. Michael runs a sandwich franchise called Le Petit Four Français. His business is located in a busy shopping centre in the food hall, but his sales were suffering because the already stiff competition was increased further when Greggs, the largest bakery chain in the UK, entered the food hall.

Michael previously didn't need to do any sales or marketing. People would come to the food hall and buy from him. He'd get a sufficient percentage of custom that he was happy with. But when Greggs came to the food hall his footfall decreased so he needed to fight back.

He duplicated the formula, and one of the first things he did was to create a series of up-sells and cross-sells on each purchase. He did this simply by cloning the Sales Accelerator Templates. By the way, up-sells and cross-sells work at the point of purchase. They are wonderful for extracting more profit out of customers, and every business should be capitalising on them, although most small and medium-sized businesses don't!

Here's what happened. In fact, here's what Michael said in his own words...

"...I have reiterated to staff the need to up-sell using the scripts, and this month we have been up three times on like-for-like sales versus last year. Amazing – thank you."

Now, remember, Michael doesn't have any sales and marketing experience or expertise. He just cloned the Sales Accelerator Templates and applied the up-sells and cross-sells to his business. Also note... his footfall had decreased yet he was up three times on sales versus the previous year.

How many of you would like to achieve a result like that?

I mean, if all you did was achieve a 50% increase on sales, wouldn't that be sweet? And remember, that's just one strategy he applied to get this result. Are you starting to see what's possible when you clone already successful strategies? It's also important to recognise that most of the tactics and strategies in The Core Asset, just like the referral system, up-sells and cross-sells work instantly. You don't have to wait for results.

So, who wants to see an example of the fill-in-the-blank Sales Accelerator Templates?

Remember, the templates and success formulas can be applied to any business.

Okay, here's the Sales Accelerator Template for what I call a Customer Welcome Letter. You use this letter to firstly ensure the sale sticks, second to reinforce why buying from you was such a great thing for them to do, and third to extend a customer special offer to them. This one strategy could be worth thousands, even hundreds of thousands to you over the coming months. In fact I estimate this one letter is responsible for generating tens of millions in extra sales for our clients over the last few years...

In my experience, very few people send a letter like this. Notice I say 'LETTER'. Our tests have proven that sending a letter delivered by the good old-fashioned postman, rather than an email, increases sales by over 300%. And here's the success formula.

Remember, the success formula acts as a checklist to ensure you get the best possible results from each tactic or strategy. The T stands for Thank the Customer. The RB stands for Restate the Benefits of why they have made such a good decision to buy from you, and the NCO stands for New Customer Offer. When those three component parts are included, it's impossible not to have a customer welcome letter that makes the customer delighted with their purchase and gives you a healthy bump in sales.

If you recall... to make it even easier for you, there are fill-in-the-blank Sales Accelerator Templates for all the strategies. In fact, I'll show you a couple of these shortly. This means you can perfectly clone each strategy or tactic to your own business, no matter what you sell, and because you're modelling success and what works already, you'll be able to launch each one with complete certainty that it will be effective. The way to look at it is like this... I've done all the hard yards for you. You don't have to learn anything. You don't have to study. It's kind of like you're getting your own degree... a first-class degree in sales and marketing that works... without the time, effort and cost. Who wouldn't want that? Right?

And that leads me nicely onto the third secret, which for many of you I know is very important.

We've already spoken about how any business can duplicate THE FORMULA and insert it into their business successfully. We've spoken about the remarkable fact that you can copy or clone success by using the success formulas and fill-in-the-blank Sales Accelerator Templates for dozens of proven tactics and strategies, and this can be done by anyone in your organisation, even someone with little or no sales and marketing expertise. Now, let's look at the last secret:

- **STAGE #7: Recap the Three Secrets and Then Segway into Your M.A.P. (Mentoring Attraction Package)**

Okay, so now you're cooking on gas! You've delivered your three secrets. Now simply recap by stating the three secrets and then move seamlessly into your M.A.P.

This is where most people struggle. Most people don't like 'SELLING'. 'Sell' is a four-letter swear word to many people, but if you're going to build a world-class mentoring business, then you are going to have to become comfortable with selling.

A good friend of mine who runs a very successful consulting franchise was telling me about one of his franchisees. The franchisee was the sales director for a company he helped to grow from £4 million to £18 million.

Part of the franchise fee goes towards getting appointments for the franchisee, and this particular guy had eight appointments set up for him. He didn't close one of them.

How could that be?

Even though he was an experienced sales director, he hadn't sold for some years, and he was out of practice. He thought that asking for the order at the first meeting was too 'salesy'.

My friend told him to follow the system which involved getting the order at the end of the first meeting, and then on his next three meetings, he did exactly that... and guess what? Yep, you guessed it. He sold the consulting service to two out of three of them.

You absolutely MUST try to get the sale at the end of your webinar. Your delegates are waiting for your 'pitch' anyway. Key, though, is how you create a bridge (or segue) from your presentation into delivering your M.A.P.

Here's how you do it...

After recapping your three secrets you then say...

> The fact is there's so much more I could share with you...
>
> I've therefore created something REALLY special to help you guys take what we've covered today and REALLY push on... So, is it okay that I share it with you now?
>
> If you're okay with that, please let me know in the question box...
>
> Alright, great.

The special package I've created for you is called <Name of Your Mentoring Service>.

- STAGE #8: Reveal Each Value Element Of Your M.A.P.

Next, you simply take the delegates through all the value elements (that we put together earlier).

As you take them through each value element, you're starting to build value and increase their desire.

Example…

So, what are you going to get when you guys invest in the Sales Accelerator Programme today?

The first thing you're going to get is 24/7 access to The Core Asset.

You're going to get complete and 100% access to the 50 current proven tactics and strategies across the five components of THE FORMULA. That includes the nine Core Elements of The T – transforming existing sales and marketing strategies, 14 rock-solid lead generation strategies, 13 conversion strategies, 11 maximising customer value strategies, and the three systems allowing you to automate and put your lead generation, conversion and maximising-customer-value components on autopilot. You get step-by-step instructions for every strategy, making it so easy for you to apply each one. The normal price for this is £797 a month.

Now, let me quickly introduce you to Adam Warner. Adam had a new accounting firm. He was a sole proprietor, and he is based on the outskirts of London in a place called Ware. Within a 15-mile radius of his office he had over 300 accountants operating... In other words, things were stacked up against him. He duplicated THE FORMULA and cloned the strategies in The Core Asset, and he has gone from strength to strength ever since. He's built a successful six-figure firm, with huge profits... bucking the trend of most accounting firms. Let me play you a short 15-second video clip with Adam explaining his results...

Remember, Adam didn't have a single ounce of sales and marketing expertise or experience. He's an accountant. If he can do it, you can, too.

Then there's Ralph Peake, he runs Luminaires, a specialist lighting company. Here's what he has said about the programme...

"Joining the programme has been one of the most successful decisions I've made.

I find the time I dedicate to the programme valuable in so many ways and totally focussed on delivering improved results for my company.

Rather than hearing and reading about incredible schemes which stood little chance of being completed, clarity and focus quickly demonstrated where and what we should put our effort into.

One strategy involved producing a case study of a recently completed project, and rather than emailing the details to

300 people, we created a list of ten targeted 'dream' clients, produced an A2 board, and had it delivered to them.

The result was 100% effective, with two meetings already taken place and one presentation due next week. Receiving four written replies of thanks and three telephone calls of thanks.

I have never experienced results like this before."

Let me just say, that a 100% response rate is, of course, NOT normal. But when you do things right and clone the strategies in The Core Asset, you will get better results than you've ever experienced before, just like Ralph is experiencing. In fact, Ralph was kind enough to send over his A2 board, which I'm showing you now. You see, as Ralph mentioned, the Core Asset includes only proven tactics and strategies that are focussed on results. There's no BS, no fluff, just actionable strategies that anyone can apply, irrespective of their business type or their experience.

And probably my favourite story is from Roberto Puth. Roberto now runs one of Germany's most successful and multi-million-euro commercial real estate businesses. He was introduced to my work way back in 2006 when he invested in one of my earlier systems.

Here's what he said...

I have known Steve since 2006 when I bought his Power Marketing course. But joining the Sales Accelerator Programme has been my single best investment of my whole career.

Not only does the Core Asset have world-class strategies, but they really work!

And are SO easy to implement.

He is also the first marketing expert I know, and I've invested in many over the years, who has strategies that work for real estate, especially commercial real estate, which is different.

For every problem you have there is a proven solution.

If you are the owner of a small or medium-sized company and seriously want to move your company and yourself to the next level, which means more profit, more business on autopilot and more personal freedom, you should absolutely invest in the Sales Accelerator Programme.

Are you getting this? Are you starting to see what's possible?

I just want to make sure you realise who this is for... It's for people just starting out in business who want to grow fast and get their new business on the right footing. It's for people with young businesses who need to quickly take the business to the next level... and it's for people with established businesses who need to scale up. And it doesn't matter what products or services you sell, or whether you sell business to business or business to consumer. It doesn't matter what country you're in... The Core Asset Vault is being used successfully by people in more than 45 different countries.

And you might be thinking you can't get started with this, because you don't have the time. That's a big mistake that will hold you back from success. Clearly, if you're not prepared to put time into growing your business, you're not that serious about growing it... and you'll keep getting the same results. We all make time to do the things that are important to us, so what you need to do if you're making a lack of time an excuse... is to elevate the growth of your business to one of your most important tasks. But also remember, The Core Asset has been created so even a junior member of staff or anyone in your organisation can do it. Seriously, there's no excuse.

So, the first thing you get is one month's 24/7 instant access to The Core Asset Vault... worth a total of £797 per month.

The second thing you're going to get – because having the tools is one thing, but, as I've just mentioned, you need to move with speed – is full access to all the proven fill-in-the-blank Sales Accelerator Templates...

- STAGE #9: Summarise and Reveal the Price

Once you've taken the delegates through your M.A.P., summarise each value element and then reveal the price.

By this time, they will be thinking their investment in your mentoring programme is going to be much higher than it is... because you've built the value, so it will be a pleasant surprise.

Also, you must tell them that this is a one-time offer. They can get this offer only on the webinar, right now.

Example...

So let's recap. When you join the programme today, you get...

- 24/7 Access to the Core Asset (£797 Value)
- Fill-in-the-Blank Sales Accelerator Templates (£397 Value)
- Your Personal Business Growth Mentor (£397 Value)
- A Monthly Scientific Marketing Makeover (£797 Value)
- And my Support Pack with the ACCELERATE Webinar and 21-Day Launch Pad Training Course (£1,294 Value)

That's A Total Value Of £3,682.

So, you'll be able to... quickly accelerate your sales and your profits, and transform your existing sales and marketing for zero extra cost. You'll be able to implement new tactics and strategies cost effectively and ensure they're the best they can be, launch them with full confidence, and do it without having to learn new stuff or study. Incidentally, I recently looked at all 50 proven tactics and strategies in The Core Asset and, amazingly, 29 of them won't cost you a single penny to implement...

Yes, 29! 29 won't cost you a penny.

You'll be able to master sales and marketing without even knowing it. And you'll finally be able to take your business where you always wanted it to go, along with the financial and personal trimmings that come with having a more successful business, and do it all regardless of your existing skills, experience or expertise.

Now, obviously, I'm not going to charge you £3,682 each month, but what I want to do now is ask you a question... How much would you pay for a single strategy that generates your business, say, an extra £1,000 of profit a month, that's, £12,000 a year... every year, of extra profit?

If I said the cost of such a brilliant asset is, say, £2000 in order to generate an extra £12,000 profit a year EVERY year, I'm sure you'd all think that's a reasonably good investment, right? After all, it really IS an investment, right? And that's the key. You're not spending money, you're investing it strategically to make more money.

Well, here's the thing... the Sales Accelerator Programme doesn't just have ONE £12,000 a year strategy... it actually has 50 of them... Imagine that for just a few seconds.

And you wouldn't be creating any of them on your own either, because the Sales Accelerator Programme includes... the Sales Accelerator Templates... your own personal Business Growth Mentor... and the Marketing Makeover Service, ensuring EVERY single strategy you create is as good as it can be.

I think you'll agree that the Sales Accelerator Programme is a truly comprehensive all-inclusive asset... and... because you guys have spent the time today to be with me, I wanted YOU to get the Sales Accelerator Programme for the best possible price....

So, for today only, we are offering the full... all-inclusive... Sales Accelerator Programme with your own Business Growth Mentor for just £397 a month, that's right... £397 per month secures £3,682 worth of value... a saving of almost £3,300 each and every month.

And when you join today... you lock in this price for as long as you subscribe to the Sales Accelerator Programme... your £397 per month will never increase... you'll never be required to pay a penny more than the £397 per month.

- <u>STAGE #10: Justify Their Investment and Guarantee Your Programme Will Bring Results</u>

Once you've revealed the price of your mentoring programme, even though it will be a pleasant surprise to many, you still need to explain that this is a drop in the ocean compared to what they'll get back by working with you.

If you can make your delegates think, "that really isn't a cost to me, it's more like a no-brainer investment, and I should easily make that back", then you've achieved the objective!

Then, completely protect their investment by giving them a money-back guarantee.

Example...

So, as I see it, you've got two choices...

Choice 1 is to do nothing. You can risk nothing and do nothing, and if you keep doing what you've always done, you're going to get the same result. Right?

I think it was Einstein who said the definition of insanity is doing the same thing time after time and expecting a different result. I've given you some good ideas today, but the chances are you won't apply them. But it is an option for you.

Or you can give it a try and invest a small amount compared to all the value included in the Sales Accelerator Programme. And just as the first option of doing nothing has no financial risk, neither does this option, because I have a philosophy in my business that if I can't make you money, I don't want yours. Now, this is a risk on my part, because even though we've made the duplicating of the formula and the cloning of the proven strategies easy for you, your results still depend on YOU to implement. So, I'm taking a big gamble on you. Nevertheless, to completely wipe out any risk on your part, we've put in place a cast-iron 30-day money-back guarantee for you.

Yep, you can try the programme out for a full 30 days, engage with your personal Business Growth Mentor, who will help you to duplicate THE FORMULA into your business and start cloning the strategies. Start transforming what you're doing right now and maybe add just a couple of strategies, and you'll see, even within a few days, how powerful the programme is. Plus, you'll be getting the 21-

day Launch Pad training course guiding you through the whole process on top of everything else.

Seriously, if you dedicate just a few hours each week, it's impossible not to more than cover this initial investment in the first week or two, and then you're in profit. But if at any time during those first 30 days, and for any reason at all if you don't like it, let me know and we'll give you your money back in full, no questions asked. Is that fair enough?

I know you're serious about increasing your sales and profits. You wouldn't have lasted this long on the call. So, do yourself, your family and your business a favour and use the programme for 30 days. Then make your decision. You've got nothing to lose and everything to gain. But don't make that decision today. The only decision you have to make today is am I going to get started? If the answer is *yes*, then go and get started, and then in a month from now ask yourself if it was worth it? If it wasn't, let us know, but it will be and you're going to love it.

- STAGE #11: Offer a 'Fast-Action Bonus'

Then, to reduce procrastination (people 'sitting on the fence') you should offer a valuable bonus to act now. Your bonus should be complimentary to your M.A.P. It could be as simple as offering the first five people who join the programme today a 'Strategy Session' with you. Or, if your M.A.P. has five or more value elements, you could just take one of the value elements out and include it as your fast-action bonus.

Example...

And I've got one last special bonus, which is only for the first 25 people...

Right now, we have several hundred people on the call, so I can't do it for all of you, but if you're REALLY serious about increasing your sales and profits and doing it quickly, for the first 25 people who join the Sales Accelerator Programme, here's what I'm going to gift you...

Before I explain, I just want to emphasise that you've got a very short window to accept this, and you won't even believe I'm going to do this – it's crazy. I'm going to walk you through this in a second, but you need to be ready for it, because when the 25 spots are gone, they're gone, so get ready you've got to act fast...

We have a special standalone sales accelerator application. It's our landmark software tool called the Sales Accelerator ROADMAP.

You're going to absolutely love this. In a nutshell the ROADMAP immediately pinpoints exactly where the lost treasure is in your business. You simply answer a few simple yes/no-type questions, and in about 30 minutes the software analyses your answers and identifies the things that will give you an instant improvement in your sales and profits.

It's taken us years to create this and literally hundreds of thousands of pounds in development costs, but it's worth it, because the ROADMAP will instantly guide you to the treasures in your business.

There isn't anything like this on the planet, and currently the ROADMAP sells for a one-off fee of £1,297. But if you're one of the first 25 people to join the Sales Accelerator Programme, I'll include the ROADMAP as part of the package. So that's an extra £1,297 thrown in... but only if you're quick.

- STAGE #12: Close the Sale Again

You have already closed the sale at least once after delivering the price of your mentoring programme. Simply tell people what they need to do to join your programme.

Example...

So, if you want to get results fast, and I know you all want that, then jump on this now. The ROADMAP is a brilliant way to quickly identify all the areas in your business which you can quickly transform and start to take advantage of the increase in sales and profits you'll get from using it every month.

And if that's the case, it's time to take action. Stop listening to me, and click on the button now showing on this page.

You'll then be taken through to our programme page where you can join thousands of others who are quickly and easily growing their sales and profits.

- STAGE #13: Answer Questions

Then simply answer any questions that have been asked during the webinar. Don't ramble on. Be succinct and keep this section to less than 10 minutes.

You should also have 3–6 'stock' questions that you have thought of that you believe are important to answer. In other words, in all likelihood, people will be thinking of asking these questions but don't, so you want to bring the questions out on the table to positively answer them.

Three questions that I will always include are...

Will this work for MY business?

What support do I get?

What else do I need to get results?

- STAGE #14: Summarise and Close the Sale

Once you've answered all the questions, simply summarise your M.A.P. and for one final time tell them what they have to do to join your mentoring programme...

Example...

Okay, we've got less than a minute left... so let me just recap one last time.

1. 24/7 Access to the Core Asset (£797 Value)
2. Fill-in-the-Blank Sales Accelerator Templates (£397 Value)
3. Your Personal Business Growth Mentor (£397 Value)

4. A Monthly Scientific Marketing Makeover (£797 Value)
5. And my Support Pack with the ACCELERATE Webinar and the 21-Day Launch Pad Training Course (£1,294 Value)

That's a total value of £3,682 for just £397 per month.

Plus, if you're one of the first 25 to join, I'll also gift you the Sales Accelerator ROADMAP worth £1,297.

As I said earlier, if you've got any more questions, simply email the team at support@thecoreasset.com. We'll also keep the chat box open for a while, so if you've got any questions just post them here, too. I want to thank you so much for joining me today. Seriously, this will change your business and your life... it's so exciting.

You just need to take that small leap of faith. I promise you, the Sales Accelerator Programme will transform what you're doing and do it quickly. So, go on. Now is the time to act. Click on the button and join now. Okay, once again my name is Steve Hackney. Thanks again, guys; I appreciate it, and I really look forward to working with you. Speak to you soon.

- STAGE #15: Add Engagement Tactics Throughout

One of the biggest challenges you face with running webinars is the fact that you don't have a crowd of people to feed off, as you would if you were running an in-person seminar.

I found this very challenging to begin with.

I love presenting, because it's such an interactive experience and you can thrive off the energy in the room. Webinars by comparison are soulless. Therefore, what you must do is use techniques that will ensure you get audience engagement.

If you don't engage your audience, many of them will simply leave the webinar or stay to the end and not join your mentoring programme. The good news is that there are some proven tactics and techniques you can use that will ramp up audience engagement...

Stories: I've already mentioned the importance of stories. You'll notice throughout this book that I've added many different stories. That's because stories are very engaging.

People love stories.

So, when you're making a point during your webinar, think of a story you can use to reinforce it.

Questions: You'll have noticed from my script examples above that I use questions a lot.

That's because by asking questions you're engaging the audience.

Think about the seminars, lectures, courses or any type of learning environment you've been in where the person delivering it doesn't use questions. We all turn off, start daydreaming and lose interest. But, when they ask questions, all of a sudden you become more engaged.

It becomes far more interesting and more enjoyable. It's exactly the same when delivering a webinar. Use questions throughout to get feedback and keep your audience completely engaged.

Interesting Slides: I'll discuss your presentation slides next, but you'll increase engagement by having stimulating and thought-provoking slides with great images and not too much text on them.

A common mistake I see is where every slide is like the previous one, and they're full of text. There's nothing more boring than that, and you'll quickly lose engagement. Figure 5.9 shows an example of an interesting and visually stunning slide...

Figure 5.9: Using Vivid Images In Your Presentation

Notice I could have just used the words, 'Then I had a breakthrough', but when you combine visually stunning images with your spoken work, people can 'see' and visualise what you're saying, so it has more impact and engages them further. We use www.shutterstock.com for all our imagery.

STEP #2: Create Your Slides

The good news is that having created your script, 50% of the work is now done. Next, you need to create your slides to support your script.

It is worth taking time over your presentation. As I mentioned earlier, you should try to make a number of your slides visually stunning with relevant images.

Don't fill your slides with too much text. The only time when I would do that is on your M.A.P. summary slides. For example, the image in figure 5.10 shows my M.A.P. Summary Slide...

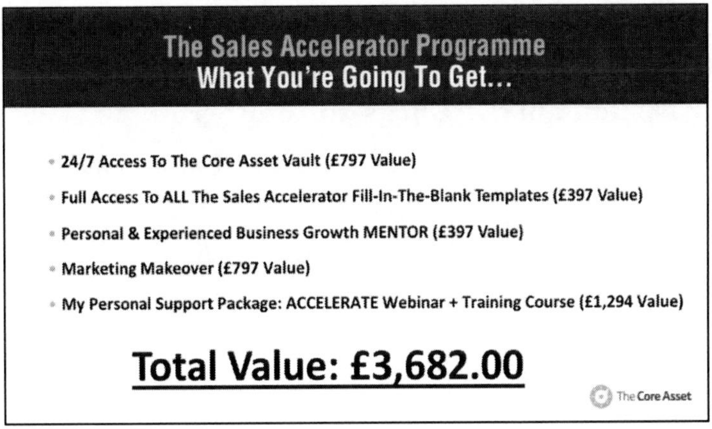

Figure 5.10: M.A.P. Summary Slide

...and the image in figure 5.11 shows my M.A.P. Summary Slide *after* I've revealed the price. Notice that both slides are text heavy, but the message is still clear, and you want your M.A.P. to be shown in full to ensure your delegates can see everything that's included.

Figure 5.11: Slide with Price Reveal

STEP #3: Build in the 'Clicks' to Your Script

Okay, so this is a painstaking part of your webinar. Having created your slides, you now need to go back to your script and add prompts for you to move to the next slide when needed (i.e. insert the 'clicks' at the right places to ensure when you deliver your script it synchronises beautifully with your presentation). That means that as you are reading your script, each time you see the word 'click' you simply click for the next slide, so your presentation moves in step with your words. Doing it this way ensures you don't risk losing your place (and flow) of your script by having to keep looking up at your presentation to make sure it's in harmony with what you're saying. Believe me, I've tried every trick in the book to get this right, and this is the best and safest way of doing it.

A good tip is to make the word 'click' bold and in capitals. Then, as you read your script it's easy to identify every click. For example, here's a piece of my script showing the clicks required...

You're going to get complete and 100% access to the 50 current proven tactics and strategies across the five components of THE FORMULA. That includes **CLICK** the nine Core Elements of The T – transforming existing sales and marketing strategies. **CLICK** 14 rock-solid lead generation strategies, **CLICK** 13 conversion strategies, **CLICK** 11 maximising-customer-value strategies, and the **CLICK** three systems allowing you to automate and put your lead generation, conversion and maximising-customer-value components on autopilot. You get step-by-step instructions for every strategy, making it so easy for you to apply each one. The normal price for this is £797 a month. **CLICK**

Obviously, once you've added your clicks, you need to do a practice run to ensure your script and slides are synchronised!

STEP #4: Select Your Webinar Platform

Now you simply need to choose the webinar platform you're going to use. There's no perfect platform, but I can certainly recommend WebinarJam. We've been using WebinarJam since it was created back in 2013, and over the years the team at Genesis Digital have made a number of enhancements and improvements.

The other leading platforms you can use include GoTo Meeting and Zoom.

STEP #5: Build Your Pre- and Post- Campaigns

Once you've chosen your webinar platform, you can then create your pre- and post-webinar campaigns.

Your chosen platform will explain exactly what's required, here, and will have the automated systems in place to make this a much easier task than you may have anticipated.

For example, you can set up...

- Reminder SMS's and emails prior to your webinar.

  Here's an example of the SMS and email we send 15 minutes prior to the webinar starting...

  SMS:

  The FORMULA Masterclass is starting in 15 minutes. Don't miss it! See you there. Regards, Steve Hackney

  Email:

  [FORMULA Masterclass Alert] We're about to start...

  "How to Add an Additional 7-Figures to Your Business in the Next 12 Months <u>Without</u> Wasting Valuable Time, Spending a Fortune on Marketing, or Having to Become a Marketing Pro"

  Hi #FIRST_NAME#,

  In just a few minutes, the FORMULA Masterclass you registered for is about to start. Please, click on the link to access the webinar room now...

Webinar Room Link: #LINK#

'See' you in the Masterclass very soon.

To your success,

Steve

P.S. If you've ever wondered WHY your business isn't growing at the rate you desire (or your efforts deserve), I can assure you it's because you're not using **'The FORMULA'**. With The FORMULA in your business, it's impossible not to accelerate the growth of your business. All is revealed in the Masterclass.

More than 26,000 businesses have proved all this can be achieved at **ZERO extra cost,** and once in place it will never stop working. **Don't miss it.**

P.P.S. Growing your business isn't rocket science, but it IS a science!

- Notification Email About the Replay

  A large number of the people who register for your webinar will either leave early, or simply not turn up. So, having the replay available is essential for you to maximise results.

- Notification Emails and SMS After the Webinar

  Whilst your aim is to sign up as many people as you can by the end of the webinar, you can still get a significant percentage of people to join your mentoring programme AFTER it. Therefore, you must follow up afterwards with a view to getting more people to join.

Having said that, you don't want it to be a never-ending follow-up campaign. I've tested this many times, and your best approach is to keep the offer open for four days in total. So, if the day you deliver your webinar is Day 1, then you should keep your offer open for another three days. For example, if you deliver your webinar on a Tuesday, the offer will close at midnight on Friday.

This follow-up sequence works well...

Email 1 – 'Thanks for Watching and Link to Join': Sent within four hours of the webinar ending.

SMS 1 – 'You Didn't Join. Any Questions?': Sent within an hour of the webinar ending (SMS is very powerful – when was the last time you ignored an SMS message on your phone?).

Email 2 – 'Q&A': Sent on Day 2.

Email 3 – 'Get Results Like These, Social Proof': Sent on Day 3.

Email 4 – 'Offer Ending Today': Sent on Day 4 (8 a.m.).

SMS 2 – Any Questions?': Sent on Day 4 (10 a.m.).

Email 5 – 'Don't Miss This': Sent on Day 4 (12 p.m.).

Email 6 – 'Last Chance': Sent on Day 4 (6 p.m.).

Here's an example 'Q&A' email we send on Day 2...

Hi ~Contact.FirstName~,

Thanks for tuning in to the **FORMULA Masterclass**.

First, an apology...

This is a long email. That's because we had so many questions at the **web event** yesterday. Things have been crazy since, with dozens of people joining on the Special Offer I revealed.

As you saw, I didn't have chance to cover all the questions, so I've collected them all and answered each one below.

If you're serious about growing your business fast, without cost or having any sales and marketing expertise, then please take 10 minutes now:

I promise it will be worth it (also, just to say, I know how important this email is to many people who tuned in, so I've put it together real quick (forgive any typos)...

QUESTION: "I don't have days and days of spare time to implement the FORMULA and the strategies. How long would you say I need to dedicate each week?" and "I am flat out running my business now. How will I find the time to implement the strategies?" (I combined these two questions)

ANSWER: I'll admit, even though I cover this in detail during the webinar, many people are naturally concerned about the time it takes to get results.

In fact, many of those people with the same fears tell us AFTER they join, that they needn't have worried, because once they see how all 50 strategies and tactics are presented with the simple Sales Accelerator Fill-in-the-Blank Templates, they can often put one of the proven tactics and strategies in play within an hour!

And, as soon as they see the results that ONE strategy generates, they just CAN'T wait to implement more, quickly building their very own business growth system.

AND remember, when you get a strategy or tactic ready to go live... you have the luxury of passing it to your own Business Growth MENTOR to check over and make sure that it's going to work right out of the gate.

So, if TIME is a challenge for you, then please don't worry... we've taken it into consideration and overcome that issue for you.

In addition to creating the tactics and strategies, you need to dedicate 45 minutes each month for your Sales Accelerator Skype call with your Business Growth MENTOR, and take time out (around 45 minutes) to tune into my monthly Accelerate Webinar.

You, of course, have to put time aside to grow your business, but also remember that once you apply one of the strategies, it's done..... and you will benefit from its results for many a year.

QUESTION: "Steve, how much is it going to cost me after I join. Do I need another budget for all these strategies?"

ANSWER: This is a great question. You'll be pleased to know that in fact 29 of the 50 tactics and strategies actually cost ZERO to create and implement...

Imagine that...

No cost whatsoever to put in place a strategy or tactic which is going to either... create you more leads... help you convert more leads into clients... and... generate more income and profit from your existing customers, clients or patients.

You see, it's not what you do that counts.... it's HOW you do it that matters, and 26,000 businesses from all over the world... are doing it the RIGHT way and growing their businesses on autopilot at minimal cost... and you can be one of them... if you're quick (see below)!

QUESTION: "How can I be sure it will work for my business?... My business IS different, Steve"

ANSWER: Look, without sounding patronising... your business ISN'T different.

Yes, it's different operationally, but when it comes to growing your business, it isn't different at all, and we've proven it with the thousands of businesses in dozens of different industries.

In fact, during the webinar I showed you numerous case studies from many different industries...

From business to business, to business to consumer.

From selling products to selling services and professional services.

From retail stores and restaurants to peculiar businesses such as 'gas fusion welding'! Anyway, hopefully you get the point.

The FORMULA doesn't discriminate.

It works for EVERY type of business.

Yours INCLUDED!

QUESTION: "How long before I will see results?", and "What is the average time to make back my initial financial investment if I implement everything by the book?" (I've put these two questions together)

ANSWER: This is simple to answer... The moment you apply one of the tactics or strategies, you'll start to get results.

That may sound hard to believe, especially if you've suffered what most of us have done over the years when you apply a tactic or strategy and, to your dismay, it doesn't work!

But we've taken all the guesswork out. We've done all the testing. Everything, and I mean EVERYTHING, in The Core Asset Vault (where all the tactics and strategies and templates are kept) is PROVEN.

The better question is this...

'How soon do YOU want to get results?'

QUESTION: "You mentioned the monthly Skype meeting of 45 mins with the Business Growth MENTOR – what if I need more help?"

ANSWER: First, each month (if you join while the special offer is still live – details below) you can send one of your tactics or strategies to your Business Growth MENTOR to undergo our brilliant *'Marketing Makeover Service'*. That will ensure you get the best possible results with all your existing and new tactics and strategies and gives you a safety net!

Second, you get my Support Package. This includes the monthly Accelerate Webinar.

Third, you can email your Business Growth MENTOR anytime, as well as email my team.

QUESTION: "What sort of experience will my mentor have?"

ANSWER: Your Business Growth MENTOR is specifically selected to join our team based on their experience, success in business and, in all honesty, they are people with the 'battle scars' to prove it.

I personally train and support them, and we work closely together to make sure all Sales Accelerator Programme members are getting the best possible results.

QUESTION: "Can I speak with Steve and/or his team before I make a decision?"

ANSWER: Of course. You can call my team anytime on +44 (0) 116 3666 325 or email them at support@thecoreasset.com.

QUESTION: "Do I really have to sign up today?", and "If I am not ready now, can I have more time to decide?", and "Will today's offer price be the same?" (I collated all these together)

ANSWER: Due to the fact that there have been so many questions, I've decided to extend the offer by another 48 hours. That will give you enough time to digest the content, watch the replay (if required), and ask any further personal questions. I hope that's okay.

QUESTION: "I am doing some of these things, so how will this system improve things for me and my business?"

ANSWER: Most established businesses (those over a year old) are doing some elements of The FORMULA and applying a few of the tactics and strategies. But you have to ask yourself three questions and be honest with the answers...

'Am I fully implementing the five components of The FORMULA?'

'How many tactics and strategies of the 50 have I implemented?'

'Of those I've implemented, how well are they working?'

In my experience, it is highly unlikely that you are fully implementing the five components of The FORMULA.

Nor will you be using more than half a dozen (or less) of the tactics or strategies.

Nor will the ones you're using be fully optimised and working to their best capacity (not using the nine Core Elements').

That means...

There's MASSIVE scope to build your business quickly when you join the Sales Accelerator Programme.

QUESTION: "The ideas are so simple. Why can't I do them for myself?"

ANSWER: You can. But how will you create them? How will you be able to model success if you don't know what success looks like, or you haven't been measuring results from other businesses who are applying them successfully?

Plus, yes, The FORMULA is simple (that's why it works so well), but even the simplest of tactics and strategies have many facets and inner workings that must be applied (hence why we created the fill-in-the-blank templates and the success formulas for each one).

Oh... and have you got the time to do all that and the money to do all the testing?

Well, you may have, of course, but why go through all the pain I had to? Make it easy on yourself.

Plus, you know that having an EXPERT working alongside you will accelerate your results even more.

Remember, as I said in the Masterclass, I don't even want your money if you can't make back your investment in the first month.

QUESTION: "Do you take the time to learn about my business and ambitions?"

ANSWER: We don't need to learn about your business, well not in detail anyway. But it is, of course, vitally important

185

we understand your goals and ambitions. That's done by your Business Growth MENTOR during your first 'Introductions Meeting'. We then make sure everything you do is geared to hitting those objectives. You need to know where you're going, right?

QUESTION: "Will MY Business Growth MENTOR visit my office, or do I travel to him/her?"

ANSWER: You and your Business Growth MENTOR conduct your monthly meetings via Skype (or an alternative such as Zoom.us). The way the programme works, there's no need to meet face to face as such. Conducting the meetings like this conserves time and maximises results for you.

QUESTION: "What tools do you have to benchmark my business before we start?"

ANSWER: If you listened to the end of the webinar, you'll notice we're offering the first 25 people who join the programme full access to our landmark software called 'The Sales Accelerator Roadmap'.

This normally costs £1,297 (one-off payment). What's so amazing about it is that by asking a number of yes/no-style questions, the software pinpoints the areas of weakness in your business from a sales and marketing and business growth perspective.

That means it tells you what to work on first, second and third, etc. I have to say, the months and months and hundreds of thousands of pounds we invested in the software has been worth it many times over.

Unfortunately, all 25 spots have already been taken but, if you join within the next 48 hours, I'll do you a big favour and include the Roadmap for you. Fair enough?

QUESTION: "How do you work with start-up businesses?"

ANSWER: As I mentioned at the start of the webinar, we work with both start-ups and established businesses.

There is a difference, though...

An established business will almost always have existing sales and marketing tactics and strategies in play. They can, of course, all be optimised to increase results instantly using the Core Elements.

Plus, an established business usually has a 'sticking point'. Typically, these sticking points (or sales barriers) are £500,000, or £1 million, or £2 million, or £5 million, or £10 million in turnover. The Sales Accelerator Programme will help an established business drive through their next sales barriers.

A start-up, by its nature, doesn't have any, or maybe only one or two current tactics and strategies. They will typically be looking to establish the business first before pushing through the sales barriers mentioned above.

Of course, The FORMULA is perfect for them, too, and gives the business its structure and foundation for growth right from the beginning, which will ensure its success.

QUESTION: "Tell me, what does the Sales Accelerator Programme include exactly?"

ANSWER: In short, during the special offer (expires in 48 hours) the Sales Accelerator Programme includes...

-- 24/7 Access to the Core Asset (£797 Value)

-- Sales Accelerator Fill-in-the-Blank Templates (£397 Value)

-- Personal Business Growth MENTOR (£397 Value)

-- A Monthly Marketing Makeover (£797 Value)

-- My Personal Support Package – Monthly ACCELERATE Webinar and Launch Pad Training (£1,294 Value)

Total value: £3,682.00, *plus* full access to the Sales Accelerator Roadmap (value £1,297).

QUESTION: "How much does it cost during the special offer?"

ANSWER: Just £397 per month.

QUESTION: "How does the guarantee work?"

ANSWER: Join today, then try the programme out for a full 30 days. Then, if in the unlikely event you decide you don't want to continue, let us know (by email), and we'll refund your entire fee, no questions asked.

QUESTION: "Can I cancel at any time?"

ANSWER: Yes. I don't believe in tying people into long-term contracts. My view is that if you're getting results, you'll never want to stop.

QUESTION: "When can I start?"

ANSWER: Right now. Join the Sales Accelerator Programme including everything above here...

Sales Accelerator Programme – SPECIAL WEBINAR OFFER >>

***

Phew, that was a lot of questions! If I somehow missed your question, or you have another, please let us know (phone: +44 (0) 116 3666 325 or email support@thecoreasset.com).

Thanks again ~Contact.FirstName~... I look forward to welcoming you into the Programme.

To your success,

Steve Hackney

P.S. In 48 hours you will never be offered this special price ever again. Join now. Take advantage of the guarantee and join with zero risk. All I'm really asking is you give the Sales Accelerator Programme a try. You can do so here.

P.P.S. Remember, growing your business isn't rocket science... but it IS a science!

Here's an example 'Last Chance' email we send on Day 4...

Subject: [LAST CHANCE] The Sales Accelerator Programme Special Offer is ending soon...

Hi ~Contact.FirstName~,

Final warning!

In less than four hours the Special Offer to join the Sales Accelerator Programme will be withdrawn forever.

I just wanted to give you one last warning...

If you're quick, you can still join the Programme and get...

- **24/7 access to The Core Asset Vault** (£797 Value)

- **The Sales Accelerator Fill-in-the-Blank Templates** (£397 Value)

- **Your Own Personal Business Growth MENTOR** (£397 Value)

- **Scientific Marketing Makeover** (£797 Value) and...

- **My Personal Support Pack: Monthly ACCELERATE Webinar and 21-Day Launch Pad Training** (£1,294 Value)...

Also, you join WITHOUT risk because of my 30-day money-back guarantee, and although you won't want to, you can cancel at any time!

That's £3,862 worth of value each month for just £397 per month.

And if you join before the special offer expires, you'll also get the Sales ACCELERATOR Roadmap worth £1,297. This amazing piece of software shows you where the 'lost treasure' is in your business and could be worth thousands to you. That's a total DISCOUNT of over 89%.

Get started now with absolutely no risk >>

To your success,

Steve Hackney

P.S. Remember, once we hit midnight, the offer expires, and **you won't be offered it again**. So, if you're sat on the fence, **join now**. Secure the substantial discount and join in the knowledge that your investment is protected by my no-quibble, 30-day money-back guarantee. **YOU HAVE LESS THAN FOUR HOURS TO TAKE ACTION.**

P.P.S. Growing your business isn't rocket science... but it IS a science!

This level of follow-up may seem extreme to you, but I can assure you, it will yield more clients for you. It's very important you 'close' the offer down on Day 4 with the three emails and SMS.

STEP #6: Set Up Payment Options

Obviously, at the end of your webinar and during the follow-up sequence, you must give your delegates payment options. In other words, you need to make it easy for them to join your mentoring programme.

I've found that the more options you provide, the more people will join your programme, so I advise you to put in place ALL of the following...

Online Payment Facility: It's now so easy to set up an online payment facility. You can use the likes of PayPal, and many others. My advice is for you to use Stripe (www.stripe.com).

<u>Offline Payment Facility:</u> As long as you have an online payment facility, you don't need an extra offline payment facility, because even if people call you to join, you or someone in your team can process their order using your online payment facility simply by visiting your 'Order Form' (see below) and entering the client's details on the form.

<u>Direct Bank Payments:</u> Some people will want to pay you directly into your bank account. Simply provide the details to them if they request that option. A great application you can use for this is GoCardless (www.gocardless.com).

You'll also need to set up an online order form. This will make the whole process of people joining your programme seamless and fully automated. People who join your programme via your online order form are agreeing to pay whatever amount you are charging and the frequency of payments.

Just a small point about the fees for your mentoring programme... I would initially advise you charge monthly, so it makes it more affordable, but you should definitely test quarterly and annual payments (or at least give clients an option to do that). This will also help fund your marketing spend (see later).

If you're looking at annual payment, we've found that giving the client effectively two months free works well. So, for example, if you charge £/$/€400 a month, then your annual payment would be £/$/€4,000, saving your client £/$/€800.

STEP #7: Set Up Order Form(s)

Once you've got your payment options in place, you can then build your order form.

You may need to get a tech person to help you with this (a good source is www.Upwork.com), but if you use Stripe and Click Funnels, for example, you can set your payment pages up yourself.

The order form is often a much-neglected part of the process. I can tell you, however, that your order form is an absolutely crucial part of your mentoring programme. It's easy to get it wrong... and if you do, you'll lose many sales. Fortunately, there are a number of proven elements you can apply that will ensure your order form works tirelessly to maximise the number of clients who sign up to your programme.

Let's go through each one...

Headline: Your order form must have a headline. The best way to do this is to simply reinforce that delegates are enrolling into your mentoring programme. Use this simple template...

Yes! I Want to Join the <Name of Your Mentoring Programme>

Contact Details: Of course, you need to get the relevant contact details from the prospect to process the order.

Support Details: It is very important that you include your telephone number and email address on the form so if people have questions they can easily contact you or your team.

What the Programme Includes: This is often missing from order forms, but again it's a crucial part of it. The good news is that all you're doing is simply listing the value elements of your M.A.P.

Site Secure Elements: To reinforce that your delegates can trust you, reinforce that their payments are secure.

<u>Guarantee and Bonuses:</u> Remember to include your guarantee and bonus(es).

Figure 5.12 shows you our order form for the Sales Accelerator Programme. As you can see, all these elements are present.

All you need to do is use this as your template and build your own order forms based on this format.

It may look simple, but so much testing has gone into getting to this point. Make sure you include all the elements above, and your order forms will optimise sales.

STEP #9: Create Webinar Landing Pages

Okay, so your webinar is now built. It will work well if you've followed the previous steps. However, you could create the best webinar ever, but if people don't watch it, then it's been for nothing.

I'll shortly talk about how you generate traffic to your webinar but, first, you need to create a number of landing pages to ensure you maximise registrations AND maximise the number of people who attend.

Here are the pages you need to create...

<u>Registration Page:</u> Your registration page is your most important page. It will either kill sign-ups or multiply them. Just like the importance of your Order Form, your registration page has similar significance. However, because it's the first step your target market will take, it's crucial you get it right.

The **Core Asset**
World-Class Mentoring

WEBINAR SPECIAL OFFER

Yes! I Want To Join The
Sales Accelerator Programme

1   BILLING INFORMATION

First Name

Last Name

Email

Street Address

Street Address Line 2 (optional)

City

State

Zip/Postal Code

United Kingdom

Phone

2   PAYMENT INFO

Credit Card Number | Month | Year | CVC

ORDER SUMMARY

Sales Accelerator Programme - Special Offer   £397.00
£397.00 / month

Subtotal   £397.00

Due Today **£397.00**

All payments are secured by 256-bit encryption

COMPLETE MY ORDER

Here's What I Get:
TOTAL VALUE £3,682...

✓ 24/7 Access To The Core Asset (£797 Value)

✓ Sales Accelerator Fill-in-The-Blank Templates (£397 Value)

✓ My Own Personal Business Growth MENTOR (£397 Value)

✓ Monthly Scientific Marketing Makeover (£797 Value)

✓ Steve's Personal Support Package - Launch Pad Training Course & Monthly ACCELERATE Webinar (£1,294 Value)

✓ NO RISK subscription with your 30-Days 'No Questions Asked' Money-Back Guarantee

✓ Easy cancellation, with no tie in - I can cancel at any time.

✓ **£3,682 VALUE For Just £397 A Month**

✓ **BONUS:** Sales Accelerator ROADMAP (£1,297 Value)

👁 **WE VALUE YOUR PRIVACY**

We will NEVER share or trade online information that you provide us (including e-mail addresses).

🔒 **SECURE TRANSACTION**

All personal information you submit is encrypted and secure with a 256-bit encryption. You can checkout with confidence.

👥 **NEED HELP?**

EMAIL US:
support@thecoreasset.com

CALL US:
+44 (0) 116 3666 325

Figure 5.12: The Sales Accelerator Programme Order Form

The good news is that your registration page will pretty much write itself as long as you've followed the previous steps (see the example in figure 5.13). Here are the important elements that make a high-converting registration page...

- <u>Sub-Headline:</u> Your sub-headline goes just before your main headline. You have two choices here: first, you can reinforce the fact that the webinar is free ('FREE Webinar Reveals...'), or you can call out your target market ('For Busy Business Owners').

- <u>Headline:</u> Use the title of your webinar as the main headline.

- <u>Main Image:</u> You should use an image with you in it!

Figure 5.13: Example Registration Page

- <u>Three Secrets:</u> List the three secrets that you're covering in your webinar (see figure 5.14 for an example).

- <u>Registration Button:</u> Include a large registration button. Your button will need to be integrated with the webinar platform you're using.

Figure 5.14: The 3 Secrets

- <u>Legal Obligations:</u> Add your company name and address, as well as links to your privacy policy, terms, and earnings disclaimer at the bottom of the page.

<u>Thanks-for-Registering Page:</u> Once someone registers for your webinar, they should be automatically forwarded to your 'Thanks-for-Registering Page'.

I advise you to place a video on this page. Your goal is simple... to reinforce how important your webinar is going to be for them and to explain what they need to do to maximise their enjoyment of the webinar.

This page should, of course, include the date and time of the webinar, and you should urge them to put the details in their diary (see figure 5.15 for a good example).

<u>Countdown Page:</u> Many of your delegates will turn up early to your webinar. For those people you need a 'Countdown Page' (see figure 5.16) that will countdown the time until you go live.

Figure 5.15: Example Thanks-For-Registering Page

Figure 5.16: Example Countdown Page

Once again, the webinar platform you choose will enable you to create this page.

STEP #10: Launch

Phew! We've covered a lot in the previous nine steps. It takes a significant amount of time and effort to get to this point when creating your webinar, but as I said earlier, it really will be worth your time, especially if you've followed my advice.

Just remember, 'good enough, *is* good enough'. Don't keep tweaking and tweaking for the sake of it. Just get launched and then you can tweak and improve as you go... then you can move to step 11...

STEP #11: Automate

I suggest you run at least half a dozen live webinars to begin with. You'll make a significant number of improvements and enhancements by doing that. Then you're ready to completely automate your webinar.

The term we use to describe this is 'Evergreen Webinar'. That means it can run 24/7, 365 days a year (if you want it to).

I would also call this 'nirvana'!

Think about it... you set up your webinar to run several times a day, seven days a week, and you don't have to attend once! It's a 24/7 sales MACHINE that never gets sick, never has a holiday and is delivered perfectly EVERY time.

After making improvements during the first six live webinars, we <u>always</u> then move to 'evergreen'.

The webinar platforms I spoke about earlier will give you the facility to automate your webinar like this.

As I explained, we use WebinarJam, and their evergreen application is called 'EverWebinar'. You basically use everything I've gone through previously, the only difference being that you can set multiple times through the day that your webinar will run, and you, of course, have to record your entire webinar. With EverWebinar, let's say your sixth run through of your live webinar is as good as you can get it, you can then select the recording of that webinar and use it as your evergreen webinar.

Alternatively, you can do a separate recording of your webinar. If that's the case, you'll need to use screen capture software such as 'Camtasia' (www.techsmith.com). These applications enable you to record voice and your screen together, so it replicates your webinar. You then simply upload your video to a video hosting platform such as 'Vimeo' (www.vimeo.com), and then insert the link into your webinar platform, and you're good to go.

3. Software Diagnostic Solution

The third Expertise First Lead Magnet is to create a 'Software Diagnostic Solution', which ultimately identifies the gaps and weaknesses in each prospective client's business or persona aligned to your mentoring skills and expertise.

I've found that this is a very effective way to acquire clients. I first started out with a 'manual' diagnostic (questionnaire). It was 52 pages long and took about two hours to go through with the prospect. Back then, creating a software programme was possible but very, very expensive, so I tolerated the manual version until it was financially viable to build a software application that would not only mirror my original diagnostic, but would significantly improve it.

If you're on a tight budget, then I suggest you first use the manual option and then, as your mentoring business grows, you can transform it into a software application.

What you need to do is create a set of closed questions (questions that require either 'yes' or 'no' answers) that will show you and your prospective clients where their gaps and weaknesses are. Psychologically, as your prospect is going through the questions with you, they will instinctively recognise that every 'no' answer is a weakness or a gap, and assuming you've positioned your skills and expertise effectively with them, they'll know you can help plug those gaps.

I've also found that providing a 'score' once they've completed the questions is another powerful approach. The prospect and you will then be able to see the level of improvement that's possible and benchmark them right now.

You can score each question the same or build in a weighting depending on the importance of each question. Whilst this is a relatively simple concept, very few people use it, and it's very powerful in terms of acquiring mentoring clients.

Our software application is called the 'Sales Accelerator ROADMAP'.

Let me explain how you put it together...

STEP #1: Align the Diagnostic to Your Results-Producing System

Your diagnostic needs to be completely aligned to your results-producing system. That means your mentoring programme MUST have a solution to each question you're asking in the diagnostic.

Our results-producing system is THE FORMULA. It has five component parts, so our diagnostic has five sections, each covering one of the five individual component parts. So, if your results-producing system has three component parts, then your diagnostic will also have three... and so on.

STEP #2: Add Closed Questions to Each Section

This is a little tricky to begin with. You shouldn't ask open-ended questions where the prospect can enter any information, because you can't then easily analyse or score their responses. Therefore, you should only use closed questions, where they can only answer 'yes' or 'no'. That means you can also give each 'yes' and 'no' a score (see next).

For example, you wouldn't ask an open-ended question such as...

"What are your top three staff recruitment techniques?"

You'd have to convert that into, say, three closed questions such as these...

"Do you use <recruitment technique 1>?"

"Do you use <recruitment technique 2>?"

"Do you use <recruitment technique 3>?"

As you can see, it just requires a slightly different approach to convert all your questions into closed questions.

First consider the key areas where your skills and expertise will significantly help most of your target market. It's obviously important that you choose your questions to help illustrate the 'gaps' that your skills and expertise can 'close' to improve your prospect's business situation. Therefore, there will be a number of questions where the likely answer is 'No'. As a guide, the value your skills and expertise can leverage should see you with around 60–70% of questions likely to be answered 'No'.

That said, please don't fall into the trap of creating your questions so they can only answer 'No' to almost all! That will obviously be deflating and will likely be seen as derogatory. Let them see that they are doing some things well... you just need to strike the right balance, otherwise there'll be no requirement for you to help them!

STEP #2: Score Each Question

As I mentioned earlier, you can score each question the same way or give certain questions a weighting depending on how important they are. Plus, you can score questions differently within each section.

Let me explain further...

Let's say you have four sections.

You have five questions in section one, ten questions in section two, eight questions in section three, and six questions in section four.

Section one is the most important, so questions in this section get 10 points for every 'yes' answer and zero for every 'no' answer.

Sections two to four are weighted the same, and every 'yes' answer gets a score of 5 and zero for every 'no' answer. Therefore, total possible scores are as follows...

Section One: 50

Section Two: 50

Section Three: 40

Section Four: 30

TOTAL Possible: 170

STEP #3: Create Score Banding

Now you know the total possible score, you can create a banding table depending on the score.

My advice is to have four or five bands...

Your Score	What This Means
0–49	Huge room for improvement
50–99	Significant room for improvement
100–139	Good room for improvement
140–170	Excellent – you'll benefit from my help, but you're already in the top 10%

Obviously, you create the banding depending on what's relevant and fair.

You're not trying to trick the prospect into getting low scores!

Be realistic and objective with your scoring and banding, and your diagnostic will be of real benefit to you and the prospective client.

STEP #4: Use the Manual Version to Iron Out Any Problems

Before getting a developer to create your software, you should use the manual version first. That will help you improve it and enable you to tweak it to get the best possible results.

It's better and more cost-effective to go to the developer with a diagnostic that's already been thoroughly tested and improved.

STEP #5: Get Diagnostic Built

Now you're in position to get the diagnostic developed into a software application. If you've built it as I've shown, you'll keep costs down to a minimum, and it will be relatively easy for any developer to build it.

Once again, I would recommend the team at Wildfire Information Systems (www.wildfireinfosys.com). At the very least speak to them and get a quote.

STEP #6: Create Landing Page

Just as you did for your other Expertise First Lead magnets, you need a landing page for your diagnostic (see example in figure 5.17).

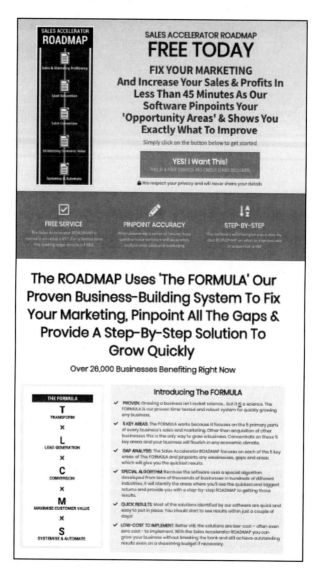

Figure 5.17: Diagnostic Landing Page

- <u>Headline:</u> Tell them that your diagnostic is free and what it will help them achieve. See the example shown in figure 5.18...

Figure 5.18: Diagnostic Landing Page

- <u>Image:</u> Show the different stages of your diagnostic in an image next to your headline.

- <u>Results-Producing System:</u> Explain how your diagnostic is based on your results-producing system, and that it will reveal all the gaps and mistakes they're making.

You can see how to do that in figure 5.19...

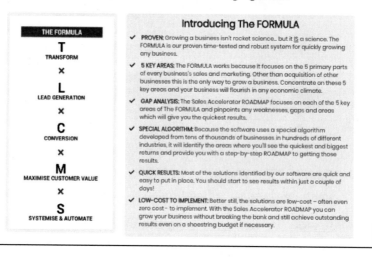

Figure 5.19: Diagnostic Explanation

- <u>The Steps:</u> Tell them the simple steps required for them to benefit from your diagnostic. see figure 5.20 for an example....

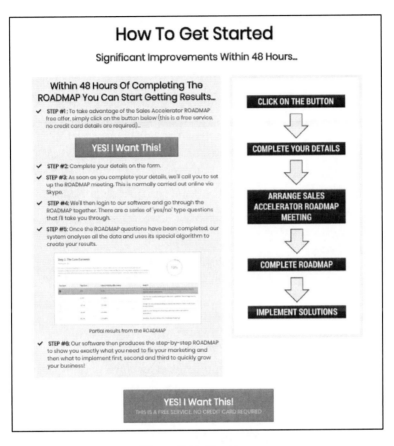

Figure 5.20: The Steps

- 'Call-to-Action' Buttons: Add your call-to-action buttons, which, when clicked, should produce a form for visitors to complete and secure their free diagnostic.

  As mentioned previously, your form should be linked to your CRM system to allow you to follow up with email and SMS.

209

Remember, you want your follow-up to be automated up until the point when you 'meet' with your prospect to go through the diagnostic (see later).

you can see an example form in figure 5.21...

Figure 5.21: Example Form

STEP #7: Thank-You Page

Once the prospect completes the form, they must go through to your thank-you page, which should include a button which links to your online diary (as explained earlier).

STEP #8: Follow-Up Campaign

You need a short follow-up campaign for people who request a diagnostic meeting. A simple email explaining what will happen next is all you need. Example email...

Subject: ~Contact.FirstName~ thank you...

Thank you for requesting a <u>FREE</u> *Sales Accelerator ROADMAP* analysis.

I'm looking forward to taking you through it and showing you exactly how to fix your marketing and accelerate the growth of your business.

Thanks again ~Contact.FirstName~.

Your Name

You also need a three- or four-email follow-up campaign for people who complete the form but don't initially book a meeting with you (nag sequence).

4. Monthly Printed Newsletter

Where do I start? You're probably reading this and thinking... "What? A printed newsletter, written monthly?... You've got to be joking, Steve."

That's a typical response when I tell people that one of the best Expertise First Lead Magnets for any business mentor is a printed monthly newsletter.

No, I'm not stuck in the 1990s! Here's why a monthly printed newsletter is such an effective Expertise First Lead Magnet...

- First, remember everything in this book is proven and, most importantly, is *working right now*!

- Second, think about it... your personal newsletter is the perfect vehicle to demonstrate your expertise.

- Third, very few mentors, coaches or consultants create and produce a monthly newsletter, so it stands out as a real point of difference for you.

- Fourth, and this is repeated several times throughout this book, direct mail (sending pieces of marketing material through the mail) is NOT dead. For those of us still using it (and we recommend all our clients use it, too) it is getting phenomenal results, better than ever before. Why? Because virtually everyone else is only using online marketing. For example, research shows we receive on average 157 emails per day and just 2 pieces of mail (USPS Marketer's Guide). Because of this, when people receive your newsletter through the mail it's welcomed and often will be read. Twenty years ago, as you know, every morning your letterbox was full of mail. Now if you get one piece of mail a day, it's a lot! So, your newsletter automatically stands out.

- Fifth, because your printed newsletter is tangible, it has a much longer shelf-life than a digital version.

- Sixth, I DON'T recommend you mail your newsletter to every prospect. It should go to your 'warm' prospects (people who you have a relationship with already, who are either clients or prospective mentoring clients). Aim for about 100 people.

- And last, because of the development of digital print over the last 10 years, you can print your newsletter for little cost.

I know having a printed newsletter may feel like it's taking you back twenty years, but I can tell you from experience and the results our mentors are getting right now that their printed newsletter is leading the way in terms of their client acquisition, positioning and the fees they command. We actually produce the newsletter for them, but let me take you through the process of what you need to make your newsletter a huge business asset for you...

But, before I do, let me tell you that I have been using printed newsletters for over twenty years. In every business I've ever had, mentoring and others, it has always been a central marketing strategy to drive the business forward. It's great for existing clients and, of course, for acquiring new clients, too. I've made more mistakes than most but, as a result, I've developed a proven system for business mentors that simply works. As you'll see, it's not rocket science, but it IS a science...

STEP #1: Decide on the Size and Number of Pages

I've tested every imaginable size and without question, the best size is US Letter Size if you're based in the USA and A4 for everyone else. The optimum length is 12–16 pages, but I don't recommend you start with 12 or 16 pages. Start with four pages and then build up to 12 or 16 pages over the course of eight months (first four months, four pages; months 5–8, eight pages; month nine onwards, 12 pages, etc.).

For our mentors, the first issue we create for them is 16 pages and then every issue thereafter is 12 pages, every month.

STEP #2: Choose the Name of Your Newsletter

The name of your newsletter is very important. It should reflect the type of mentoring services, skills and experience you provide. Don't try to be clever with it. We have a saying here in the UK... 'it does what it says on the tin'. That means just say it as it is. And you should do so!

For example, if your area of expertise is *leadership*, don't call your newsletter 'Growth' or something weird like 'Envision'. Name it something like, 'The Leader' or 'Empower' or 'Leaders Are Created'. Do you see the difference?

STEP #3: Get a Designer to Create Your Template

In this day and age, with all the various programmes and apps, we can all begin to think we are accomplished designers. Frankly, we are NOT. Graphic design is a professional skill, and when it comes to your newsletter design, unless you are a trained designer, pay a one-off fee to a graphic designer to create the design template. Once you have the template, you'll use that same template for ALL your monthly issues. Believe me, a small fee paid to a professional designer will pay you back handsomely, and your newsletter will look stunning.

You'll need the following pages designed along with the various features listed (see figure 5.22 showing the main elements)...

- **Front Page:** This is your most important page. These are the elements you MUST include (tell your designer they must include these features)...

    1. Nameplate: This is the top part of the front of your newsletter. It includes the name of your newsletter and other elements, as detailed below.

    2. Newsletter Name: This should be the most prominent part of the page and really stand out.

Figure 5.22: Newsletter Front Page Main Elements

3. <u>Tagline:</u> Goes under your newsletter name and should explain what the theme of your newsletter is.

4. <u>Contact Details:</u> Add your contact details (name, address, email, web address, phone number, etc.).

5. <u>Issue Number:</u> You can of course date your newsletters rather than use issue numbers. Also, it's VERY IMPORTANT to give your newsletter a value. This increases the perceived value of it. Any amount from £/$/€57 to £/$/€197 per month works well.

6. <u>Lead Article Headline:</u> All your articles must have a powerful headline to drag the reader into reading each one.

7. <u>Author:</u> Since the whole purpose of your monthly printed newsletter is to establish your expertise, make sure you add your name to each article.

8. <u>Head Shot Photo:</u> Include a smiling photo of yourself (dressed appropriately) on the front page. This helps people to connect with you.

9. <u>Drop Capital:</u> Start your articles with a 'drop capital'. They are proven to direct readers into your articles and start reading.

10. <u>Table of Contents:</u> Provide the headings of all your articles in a table of contents.

11. <u>Folio (footer):</u> Add your differentiator to the bottom of each page.

- **Inner Pages:** You just need an inner left-hand page and an inner right-hand page designing. These are the elements that are important (see the example in figure 5.23)...

  1. Modified Nameplate: Reduce the depth of the nameplate and just include the name of your newsletter along with the tagline.

  2. White Space: It's hard to read text on coloured or dark backgrounds, so make sure the main article space is white or a light colour.

  3. Folio (Footer): Add your differentiator to the bottom of each page.

- **Back Page:** Your back page is also a very important page. When your newsletter is delivered it may land front page up or back page up (as you'll see below, you'll be putting your newsletter in a clear plastic 'envelope' rather than a normal envelope, so your newsletter will be seen). Therefore, your back page also needs to be alluring, just like your front page (see the example in figure 5.24)...

  1. Modified Nameplate: As above.

  2. White Space: As above.

  3. Expertise First Lead Magnet Promotion: Your back page is a prime spot to promote one of your other Expertise First Lead Magnets. This is VERY IMPORTANT. Prospective clients who you send your newsletter to must be guided to one of your Expertise First Lead Magnet landing pages so you

can turn them into a lead and then convert them into a mentoring client.

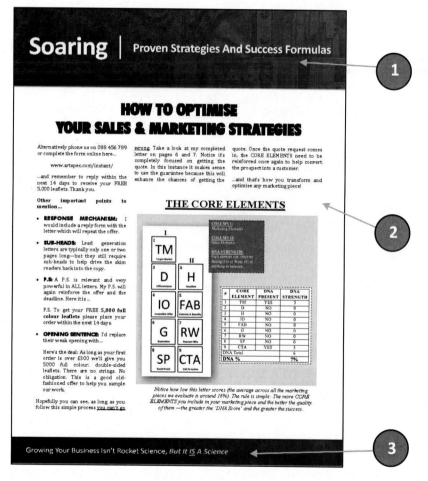

Figure 5.23: Newsletter Inner Page Elements

218

4. <u>The Last Word Article:</u> It's important to also include an article on the back page (it should NOT be all promotional). Then you've got a much better chance of people reading your Expertise First Lead Magnet promotional piece.

5. <u>Publisher Details:</u> You are the publisher of YOUR newsletter, so make that clear. Add your contact details again.

6. <u>Folio (Footer):</u> As previous.

STEP #4: Plan Your Content

Obviously, the number of pages you have will dictate the number of articles you can include. Here's a guide to the number of articles I'd include, depending on the total number of pages in each issue...

- **4 Pages:**

  Article 1 – Pages 1 and 2

  Article 2 – Page 3

  Last Word Article – Page 4

- **8 Pages:**

  Article 1 – Pages 1 and 2

  Article 2 – Pages 3–5

  Article 3 – Pages 6–7

  Last Word Article – Page 8

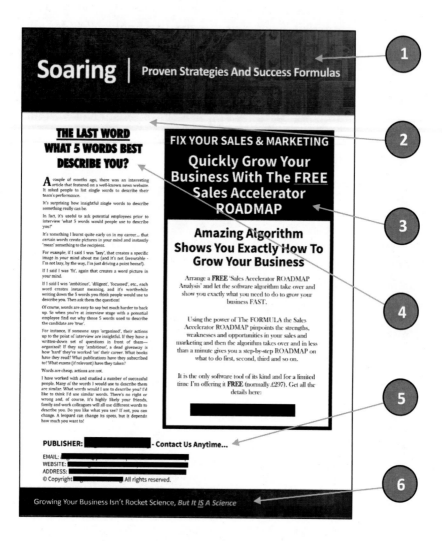

Figure 5.24: Newsletter Back Page Elements

- **12 Pages:**

  Article 1 – Pages 1 and 2

  Article 2 – Pages 3–5

  Article 3 – Pages 6–8

  Article 4 – Pages 9–11

  Last Word Article – Page 12

- **16 Pages:**

  Article 1 – Pages 1 and 2

  Article 2 – Pages 3–5

  Article 3 – Pages 6–7

  Article 4 – Pages 9–11

  Article 5 – Pages 12–15

  Last Word Article – Page 16

The content of your articles simply needs to be based around 'How To…'. In other words, you're telling your reader how to accomplish a certain tactic or strategy based around your skills and expertise.

Don't be worried about giving away your secrets. There are very few people who will act on your advice and, of course, they would need your help to implement the tactic or strategy to a high level. Don't hold back with your information. Be very giving, just like I am with this book. I promise you, the more you give… the more you'll get.

At least one article should also include a link to one of your Expertise First Lead Magnet landing pages.

STEP #5: Add Images, Examples, Photos, Diagrams, etc.

The good news is that you don't have to cram your newsletter full of written content. In fact, I strongly advise against that. You need to break up your newsletter and articles with images, examples, photos, diagrams, charts, illustrations and so on.

Generally speaking, your imagery should take up around 30% of your newsletter!

STEP #6: Proofread

Once you've written the newsletter, get someone else to proofread it for you and then make any necessary changes.

STEP #7: Print

Once you've approved the final version, you can then send it to the printers. Look for a local printer (they will be a good mentoring client prospect for you!). Print in full colour (there's very little difference in cost between colour and black and white, and colour, of course, looks far more professional and better conveys value.

STEP #8: Mail

As I mentioned earlier, we've found that placing your newsletter in a clear plastic envelope gets the best results. An added benefit is that they are extremely cheap compared to normal paper-based envelopes! Place a mailing label on the front of the plastic newsletter and then mail either first or second class.

STEP #9: Send Monthly

Finally, plan your content creation so you produce one issue per month. Choose a particular week in the month to send your newsletter and stick to it (this consistency breeds familiarity and people will look forward to receiving it). For example, send each issue during the first week of each month.

Then let your newsletter work its magic!

***

Now, with at least one Expertise First Lead Magnet in place, you can start to fill your funnel(s). In other words, you can begin to drive traffic to your landing page(s).

Before I reveal the best sources of traffic for you, I want to discuss a very important principle with you. I call it the *'1 For 1'* principle... and it's crucial when growing a world-class mentoring business.

The '1 For 1' Principle

This is arguably THE most important part of this book, and if you master the *'1 For 1'* principle, you'll be astonished at the rate of growth you can achieve with your business.

So, what is the '1 For 1' principle?

It concerns what you spend on, and what you get back from, your lead generation traffic building activity.

Quite simply, it means if you spend one pound, dollar or euro, you should strive to get at least one pound, dollar or euro back.

In fact, I'd go one step further and say your aim is to spend one pound, dollar or euro and get at least one pound, dollar or euro back in the SAME month.

Why is this so important?

Well, the secret to lead generation and scaling your mentoring business is being able to generate leads without restricting your budget... and, if you think about it, if for every one pound, dollar or euro you spend, you're getting at least that back each month, then you don't have to worry about cash-flow or even having a marketing budget.

And, because most of your mentoring clients will pay you monthly, as long as you retain them (see later) every month thereafter you're significantly increasing your return on investment. For example, if you keep your clients on average for 12 months, then your return on investment is 1100% (11 times your initial investment in the first month).

Now, if you think about that for a moment, even a less than 1 For 1 return will still be a great return for you, but you then need to consider cash-flow, and I'd prefer you not to have to do that... and as long as you follow my advice, you won't need to accept anything less than a 1 For 1 return in the same month.

Once you master this one principle, it means it doesn't 'cost' you a single penny to generate clients, which in turn means you can scale your mentoring business very quickly.

Without doubt, generating leads is <u>the</u> most expensive part of any marketing. So, if you can acquire clients at break-even in the first month, you can keep doing it, and as each month follows the recurring income of the clients you acquire in the previous months keeps multiplying.

Here's a simple but absolutely realistic example...

Let's say each mentoring client pays you £/$/€400 per month for one hour of your time. And it costs you £/$/€400 to acquire each client and, let's say, in month one and each month thereafter, you invest £/$/€800 in your lead generation activity. Remember, you're recovering your investment each month, because you're getting 1 For 1. The table in figure 5.25 shows how it looks over a six-month period...

Lead Generation Investment	Return In Month	New Clients Acquired	Total Clients	Total Monthly Income
800	800	2	2	800
800	800	2	4	1,600
800	800	2	6	2,400
800	800	2	8	3,200
800	800	2	10	4,000
800	800	2	12	4,800

Figure 5.25: The '1 FOR 1' Principle

Interesting, eh? And you can, of course, invest more each month to scale faster! But if it was this easy, everyone would be doing it, right?

So, why are only a minute percentage of people able to get these sorts of results from their lead generation activity? Well, it's because they don't put in place what I've been taking you through. Or they do put it in place, but it's ineffective because they've done it wrong.

Now, I obviously don't know what your personal objectives are and, as we discussed earlier, it's not just about the money, but most people would be happy to work 12 hours _per month_ and generate just under five thousand pounds, dollars or euros _per month_... which you'd be doing from Month 6 onwards, even if you stopped your lead generation activity, using this example. Agreed?

This is just one small section of this book but, as I said, if you master this one principle, you can grow your business and scale it very quickly. This is NOT rocket science, but very few people grasp the principle of 1 For 1, and fewer still make it happen.

Further, I'm going to show you how you can change the dynamic so that instead of _just_ 1 For 1, you're getting 1 For 2, 1 For 3 or 1 For 4, or more. In other words, for every pound, dollar or euro you spend, you're getting back, two, three or four times that. And before you start thinking, "all this sounds wonderful in theory, Steve, but it can't happen in reality", I can assure you that many of my mentors around the world are doing exactly this. None of this is BS. It sounds almost unbelievable that the concept of 1 For 1 or better can be done, but when you set your mentoring business up as I'm explaining and you follow the steps I'm taking you through, it's achievable. But, you do have to understand that EVERYTHING I'm teaching you in this book is making the principle of 1 For 1 happen.

It's not just about getting your lead generation to work like a well-oiled machine. You also have to get your pricing right. You also have to get your M.A.P. right. You also have to convert your leads into clients. You also have to retain them. And, not least, you also have to generate results for them....... and so on. In many respects I'm giving you the platform to ensure you can deliver on the principle of 1 For 1, because that is the crux of building a world-class mentoring business, but everything has to work in harmony for that to be achieved.

Does that make sense?

To be frank, achieving 1 For 1 is the easy part. It's everything else that will take you time and effort. And that's why only a small percentage of people are able to achieve the results I'm talking about, simply because they don't have the work ethic or knowledge to put all the other pieces of the jigsaw together.

Now, I don't know how determined you are. I don't know what your work ethic is. I don't know how successful you want to be. I don't know how committed you are to achieving results. But, what I do know is that you want to create a successful mentoring business (you wouldn't have read this far if that were not the case).

...and this book IS giving you the knowledge, you just need to apply the time, effort and commitment to put all the steps in place. Do that, dear reader, and you'll build a truly world-class mentoring business that gives you everything you ever wanted and more... because you will achieve 1 For 1... and when you do that, nothing will stop you.

Now, remember, you have to put all the steps in place that I'm revealing in this book, not just the various lead generation elements in this chapter. However, since ALL of the lead generation activity you apply will cost you either time or money or both, you have to choose the traffic generation tactics wisely, and I'm going to take you through the tactics that will bring you the biggest return for your time, effort and cost.

Oh, and if you're thinking that not every lead generation tactic is a cost, that's flawed thinking. It's absolute rubbish to think that you can drive traffic without it costing you in <u>time,</u> or <u>money,</u> or both.

For example, tactics such as search engine optimisation or social media activity, which many people believe are 'FREE', simply are NOT. If you're doing them yourself it's taking time, and you must attach a COST to that. Okay, it's not a real cost in terms of spending money, but it is a cost in terms of your time. However, I'm not saying don't undertake activities which only cost you in time, and I'm shortly going to reveal a very powerful tactic you can use that doesn't cost you in hard cash, but will take up your time and, especially in the early days, this is a worthwhile 'sacrifice' to make.

What follows are what I consider the best tactics you should use to generate leads for your mentoring business. How good you become at each of them will determine how well you achieve 1

For 1. But, if you follow everything in this book you'll 'de-risk' the importance of mastering these lead generation tactics, because everything else is working in your favour, too.

And, before I reveal the tactics, let me say, you DON'T have to master any of them. You can pay other people to do them for you by simply outsourcing them to experts in each lead generation tactic.

Plus, I just want to tell you that we are SO lucky now when it comes to lead generation. When I was starting out twenty-plus years ago, generating leads was so much harder. The internet was only just getting started, so we could rely only on the likes of print advertising, direct mail, telemarketing, radio and TV. These traditional tactics are still relevant today but, because of the development of the internet, we now have superb alternative platforms and media channels we can use, such as Google, Facebook, YouTube, Instagram, LinkedIn, and so on.

Better still, these platforms have developed highly-sophisticated targeting algorithms using artificial intelligence machines that learn day by day, making it even easier for you to target the RIGHT people... your exact target market.

So, what follows are the tactics I know work exceptionally well when it comes to generating leads for mentoring businesses. I'm not going to take you through the exact steps required to master each tactic, but I'll give you enough 'inside' information so you can grasp each of them. Some are easier than others to apply, and almost all of them will eat into your spend if you're not careful, so I implore to use my 'Minimum Risk Formula'...

The Minimum Risk Formula

Before I introduce the Minimum Risk Formula, let me tell you another story...

Whilst I was playing for Leicester Tigers, I set up another business with a fellow player. Matt Poole played in the second row alongside Martin Johnson (England's World Cup–winning captain). He, like me, was very entrepreneurial, and in 1997 it was an exceptional year of sporting success for the city of Leicester.

Tigers won the domestic cup (The Pilkington Cup), Leicester City F.C. won the League Cup, Leicestershire County Cricket Club won the County Championship and Martin Johnson was picked to captain the British and Irish Lions in South Africa in the summer. It was an unprecedented and never-to-be-repeated season for the three Leicester clubs.

But no one was doing anything to celebrate this success. So, Matt and I created a company called Top Table Corporate Events Limited, and our first event would be a dinner to celebrate Leicester's astonishing sporting success in 1997.

We called the dinner The Captains Celebration Dinner (see the brochure in figure 5.26).

We arranged for all the club captains to be present at the dinner... Dean Richards (our captain), Steve Walsh (Leicester City's captain), James Whitaker (Leicestershire County Cricket captain), as well as the newly appointed British Lion's captain, Martin Johnson.

Figure 5.26: The Captains Celebration Dinner Brochure

Don't miss your opportunity to share in this success at the Captains Celebration Dinner

What a year it's been. Never before has one City achieved so much in the Nation's three highest profile sports.

- **Leicester City 1996/97 Coca Cola Cup winners**
- **Leicester Tigers 1996/97 Pilkington Cup winners**
- **Leicestershire County Cricket Club 1996 Britannic Assurance County Champions**
- **Martin Johnson named as captain of the British Lions**

Leicester will probably never again experience this level of achievement in one year. So why not join the victorious captains Steve Walsh, Dean Richards, James Whitaker and Martin Johnson for dinner celebrating their teams' unprecedented success.

Invite your customers, staff and friends to this memorable celebratory event. Book your places now to avoid disappointment.

Where better to celebrate this unique achievement than at Leicester City's highly acclaimed Carling Belvoir Suite.

- The evening kicks off with a reception between 7.00 and 7.30pm on Monday August 11th when you will be greeted with a complimentary drink.

- Enjoy a sumptuous 3 course dinner, a bottle of red and white wine at your table and listen to the Captains recollect their unique successes.

- The evening will be light heartedly hosted by ex England cricketer and highly acclaimed after dinner speaker, Geoff Miller.

- Just when you thought the evening couldn't get any better sit back and enjoy a video, highlighting the moments that made the last 12 months so memorable for each club.

- The evening will be a mixed event. Dress code; Lounge Suits and Evening Dresses.

*Putting something back into the community especially after such success is important. Therefore all proceeds from a raffle and auction will go to the **Football World Cup for Learning Disabilities**.*

world cup 98

Figure 5.26: The Captains Celebration Dinner Brochure

We then approached each of the clubs and asked them all if they would happily give us the contact details of all their corporate sponsors, box holders and advertisers, and to our surprise, they all agreed (that just wouldn't happen now, because of data protection).

In other words, we had the perfect target market. We had the contact details of every business that was supporting each club. In all, we had just under 10,000 business contacts... each and every one of them an avid sporting investor and fan.

We put the whole evening together, which would be held in Leicester City's new multi-million pound stand in the 'Carling Belvoir Suite'. Tickets were £49.95 each, and there were 300 tickets available.

I created a simple mailing piece (shown in figure 5.26), and we mailed the entire list. We sold out within three days. The sponsorship money we received from the five major sponsors paid for the mailing and the cost of the food, etc. Just in ticket sales we generated £14,985, which was effectively our profit from the evening.

It was a major success, but what happened next put the company out of business (there are two important lessons)...

Following the success of the Captains Dinner, Matt and I created the Leicestershire Sporting Luncheon Club. We figured that on the back of the success of the dinner and the fact that outside London, Leicester was the sporting capital of the UK at the time, there was a real desire to have a sporting luncheon club.

Matt and I were so excited.

I wrote a two-page sales letter, and we both 'fell in love with it'. So much so that we decided to mail the entire list of 10,000 that we had acquired from all the clubs.

That mailing cost just over £15,000 to print and mail. That was basically all our profit from the Captain's Dinner. Having written the letter, fallen in love with it and anticipating 150 members joining the club at £349 per year (£297 for the lunches and £50 per year membership fee), it would be a decent business right from the outset, especially when adding sponsorship monies.

It simply couldn't fail... so, as I said we sent the mailing pack out in April 1998 (see the two-page sales letter shown in figure 5.27).

Then we waited (if you've ever used direct mail, you'll know the wait between sending the mailing piece out and getting the first responses is agonising).

Then three days later we got our first order... and the second... and the third.

Then on the fourth day we got two more orders.

Then guess what happened?

That was it. We didn't receive another order. Not one more.

Our amazing sporting luncheon club had a grand total of five members.

It was a complete disaster.

Corporate Events Limited

Introducing Leicester's only Sporting Luncheon Club

Membership is restricted to 150 places... So hurry if you don't want to miss out!

Dear Fellow Sports Enthusiast

I'll get straight to the point. We live in a city that thrives on its sporting prowess. In fact we're sporting "nuts." That's why we've started Leicester's **only** Sporting Luncheon Club. It's for busy business people like you who enjoy sport and like mixing with people who have similar fervent sporting interests. But it's like no other Sporting Luncheon Club...

First and foremost it's a Member's Club. Once we reach 150 Members our doors will close. No other Memberships will be on offer. You'll be part of a very exclusive Sporting Club. Jealousy will be rife amongst your friends and business colleagues.

Of course being a member of such a prestigious Club has many other benefits. You'll receive...

- **Ten exquisite 3 course lunches** throughout the year at Leicester City's Gary Lineker Suite. You only pay for your drinks. There are no hidden extras!

- **Hilarious sporting guest speakers** at every luncheon. We've hand picked the first three - Geoff Miller, Brian Voyle-Morgan and Gareth Chilcott. Each one is accompanied by the brilliant compere Dave Ismay. However, as it's your Club we're giving you the opportunity to choose the next seven guest speakers from our specially selected group of sought after speakers.

- **A limited edition print** of only 200 copies - by Leicester's No.1 sporting artist - Tony Booker. Framed and signed by the three title winning Leicester captains - Steve Walsh, Martin Johnson and James Whitaker - your personalised print will be branded to your specification with, for example, your name and company name. This alone is worth at least £150.00.

- **A free copy of the best selling golf video** "The Swing - A lesson for Life" by John Cook and Mark Wallace - two of Europe's finest golf coaches, worth £12.99.

- **Excellent networking opportunities** with other members. We aim to compile an index of all the Members' products and services to encourage business interaction. You'll easily pay for your membership with business generated from the relationships you forge with other members.

Please read on

Figure 5.27: Sporting Luncheon Club Sales Letter

- **Member's discount scheme.** Exclusively for Members, a discount scheme for goods by Rolex, Adidas, Sony, Panasonic, Philips, Canon, LG, Kenwood, Cartier and many others. These will be available to you - and your friends and family - at prices well below those on the High Street. Just one call to our special ordering point will enable you to claim these special discounts. <u>Another opportunity to save the price of your membership!</u>

- **Practical Golf tips.** John Cook our golf adviser will be on hand at every lunch to provide you with practical golf tips. John is a four times European Tour winner and official PGA Coach to the Golf Union and a number of European Tour players.

- **Your very own exclusive member's tie** - wear it with pride.

- **Your membership is fully transferable.** If you can't make a date, treat someone else! Of course if you have more than one Membership you have the added bonus of inviting any client, prospect, colleague or friend to come along with you. This flexibility is very important - we want your membership of the Sporting Luncheon Club to be another source of income for your business!

You get all these benefits and ten lunches for only £299 plus £50 membership (renewable every year).

<u>So, how do you join this exclusive Sporting Luncheon Club?</u> All you have to do is fill in and return the tear-off slip enclosed. You can then fax it to us on **0116 251 5510**, or place it in the envelope provided (no stamp required). Quicker still, confirm your Membership by calling us direct on **0116 253 0920**. Hurry if you don't want to miss out.

Your 'Better Than Risk Free' Guarantee. Membership to the Luncheon Club has a 'better than risk free' guarantee. If after the first lunch you're in any way dissatisfied with any aspect of the Luncheon Club, I'll refund <u>all</u> your money - no quibble. Furthermore, you can keep the free golf video worth £12.99. So at worst you'll have had a free lunch, listened to Geoff Miller and received a free video worth £12.99 - I can't be fairer than that!

So don't delay. Don't put this letter down and say to yourself "yeah, this sounds great, I'll get in touch in the next couple of days." Do it now or you could miss out. I don't want to have to say to you "Sorry, we're full up!"

Thanks for your time.

Regards

Steve Hackney

*NB. **The first lunch is on Friday May 21st**. 'Phone us now on **0116 253 0920** or fax us on **0116 251 5510** to reserve your membership. Don't forget membership is restricted to 150 and also remember that if after the first lunch you're not totally satisfied, we'll refund all your money, and you can keep the free golf video worth £12.99. There really is nothing to lose!*

Figure 5.27: Sporting Luncheon Club Sales Letter

And since we wasted all £15,000 of profit in the business on that one mailing, Matt and I decided to call it quits and close the business.

So, why tell you this story now?

Well, as I explained, there are two very important lessons to be learned from it that are as relevant today as they were back in 1998.

Firstly, don't ever 'fall in love' with your marketing. This is a very dangerous thing to do, because, as it did with Matt and I, it lulls you into a false sense of security. What _you_ think of your marketing is absolutely irrelevant. Let your target market tell you how good it is from the number of leads and clients you generate! That's the acid test, _not_ what you think about it!

Secondly, no matter how good you think your marketing is... no matter how good you think your mentoring service is... no matter how unique your service is... you must **TEST SMALL**.

Think about it... if Matt and I had first sent a test mailing to, say, a thousand people on the list, that would have cost us around £1,500, but the results would have told us a huge amount about the campaign and the luncheon club concept. That test mailing would have produced one or two members at most, so it would have forced us to change the offer or maybe even ditch the concept completely, but we'd still have about £13,000 left in profits, and you could do a lot with that kind of money back in 1998!

As a result of this experience, I vowed I'd never risk everything ever again, no matter how good the marketing and the product or service was. I would test small. I would use what I call the *'Minimum Risk Formula'*. In other words, I would spend as little as I could to give me a statistically valid result, and based on results that would then determine the next steps.

If the test went well, I would then gradually increase the budget each time so I would never unnecessarily financially expose myself. If the test went badly, I would re-evaluate... and so on.

You lose nothing using the Minimum Risk Formula. If your first test works well, it's highly likely your second test will work well too, and so on. If your first test doesn't work well, it's highly likely if you don't change anything, your second and third tests will fail, too.

So, the moral of the story is twofold... don't ever fall in love with your marketing, and ALWAYS use the Minimum Risk Formula to test small.

That way, you are never going to expose yourself financially. So, make yourself and me a promise that you'll only ever use the Minimum Risk Formula. And on the back of your promise, let's now start to take a look at the lead generation tactics that I recommend you use, starting with a little refresher...

Reaching Your Target Market and Filling Your Funnel

As explained at the start of this chapter, there are numerous tactics you can use to approach your target market. You're looking for the tactics and platforms/media channels where your target market can be easily reached. Now, it's highly likely that the three lead generation tactics I'm going to discuss with you will apply to your target market, but it's important you also use any other tactics and platforms/media channels that you can use to reach your target market (as mentioned earlier).

The fact is, as long as you put in place everything I'm taking you through for each tactic, whilst having slightly different advertising or marketing nuances, the same four principles apply...

1. Use a tactic that enables you to cost-effectively reach your target market.

2. Drive the target market to your landing page (fill your funnel).

3. The landing page then converts the traffic into a lead.

4. Your conversion system then takes over (see next chapter).

The ONLY thing that's different in this whole approach is the type of lead generation tactic you're using. EVERYTHING else will pretty much stay the same.

Here are the three tactics you should use...

Businesses That Show 'Growth Intent'

I wish I'd figured this tactic out when I first started. It's so simple yet is very successful. Outside our community of business mentors, I don't know of anyone else doing this (until I released this book, of course!).

What follows is a proven and very successful tactic that will cost you time but NO money (unless you pay someone to do it for you).

No matter what your mentoring service is. No matter what your skill and expertise is. No matter where in the world you are… the best types of clients to work with are those who are ambitious, those who are constantly looking to grow, those who are intent on building a more successful business. These are the types of businesses that you'll always love working with.

So, how do you find businesses like that?

It's extraordinarily easy!

All you do is the following…

1. *You look for businesses which are spending money on their marketing and advertising*: This includes any business in your target market that…

   - is placing ads in your local newspapers, business directories, magazines, small local pamphlets, etc.

   - is sending any direct mail (anything through the post – letters, brochures, flyers, etc.);

   - is advertising on Google (you're looking for businesses placing 'sponsored ads' in the top four positions on the page of the search results for their type of product or service);

   - is sending you any emails;

   - and so on.

2. *You look for businesses which are demonstrating growth.* This includes any business in your target market that...

- is featured in relevant press releases in your local newspapers and magazines;

- is advertising for new staff (job boards, job section in newspapers, etc.).

The Process:

- Identify the businesses using the approach above.

- Visit their websites to find the name(s) and email addresses of the people you specifically need to target (usually the CEO, Managing Director, Director, etc., but you will know who your best target is).

- If you can't find their name on the website, call and ask for it.

- Create an email promoting your Expertise First Lead Magnet. You must direct them to your landing page.

- Email each business (ideally you should create a sequence of emails – one email will never yield the results that a *campaign* will produce).

- If you have more than one Expertise First Lead Magnet (and, as I've said, you should have multiple ones), then start your sequence of emails promoting your primary Expertise First Lead Magnet and, for those who don't request it, put them in another sequence for your other lead magnet(s).

This takes time to set up but, remember, once in place (other than tweaking and improving each email) you don't have to re-create them.

For example, see figure 5.28 showing the campaigns we set up for our mentors. The campaigns with a black box around them specifically promote the lead magnets we have in place for them.

Don't be alarmed at the complexity of this. We've developed this campaign structure using InfusionSoft (Keap) over several months. Start with one campaign and then build upon it...

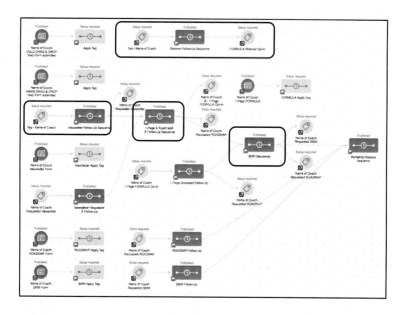

Figure 5.28: Email Campaign Structure

- You should write four emails for each Expertise First Lead Magnet. Figure 5.29 includes a screenshot showing you the emails in our monthly newsletter sequence (the emails are shown as envelope icons and the clock icons show the time delay between each email)...

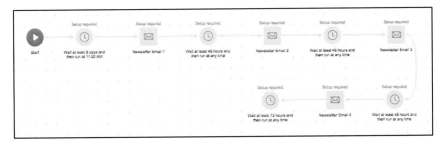

Figure 5.29: Monthly Newsletter Email Sequence

And, here's an example email from this sequence. Notice the links go directly to the newsletter landing page...

Subject: The business growth newsletter delivered to your door...

Hi ~Contact.FirstName~

I don't know about you, but I like reading books and magazines rather than reading them online.

I'm therefore thrilled to reveal that my new business growth newsletter titled, "**Name of Newsletter**" is available to you for **FREE,** and I'll even mail it the good old-fashioned way, so it comes through your letterbox every month as a printed physical copy.

If you're looking to multiply your sales and profits, and to increase the value of your ~Contact._Industrytype1~ business, you'll love my newsletter.

I get great feedback from everyone who gets it through their letterbox each month!

My first issue includes...

- **Page 1: The FORMULA** – Applying the Proven Business Growth System to Your Business

- **Page 3: Optimisation** – How to Multiply the Results From ALL Your Marketing Strategies

- **Page 8: Acres of Diamonds** – Proven and Easy Strategies to Maximise Your Sales and Profit From Your Clients, Customers or Patients

- **Page 10: Love Thy Customer** – Creating a 'Customer Offer Letter' to Quickly Increase Sales

- **Page 12: Online Mastery** – Creating a Powerful, FREE 'Lead Magnet'

- **Page 16: The Last Word** – What Five Words Best Describe You?

Each monthly issue of **"Name of Newsletter"** will be jam-packed full of easy-to-apply tactics and strategies that will have a major impact on your business.

There are no strings.

All you have to do to get the newsletter delivered to your door for FREE each month is complete your address details here...

>> Complete Your Address Details

Thanks again ~Contact.FirstName~.

To your success,

Full Name | *Business Growth Mentor*

P.S. My newsletter comes with three simple promises...

I promise to deliver a stimulating newsletter full of thought-provoking business growth strategies unlike anything you'll have read before... I promise everything in it will be proven... and I promise you'll be able to apply the tactics and strategies quickly and cost effectively. Get your **FREE copy** delivered to your door every month simply by telling me where to send it...

>> Complete Your Address Details

What I've just revealed to you, is the ONLY strategy I recommend you use that doesn't involve paying for your traffic. My advice is to dedicate a week or two to identifying as many local businesses as you can (within say a 10-mile radius of your home or office) and then to spend a couple of hours per week adding new businesses to your funnel. This type of activity shouldn't stop!

It is painstaking work, especially getting the details of each business, but of course it's simple work that can be outsourced. Either get one of your children or find someone on sites such as Upwork (www.upwork.com) to do the work for you.

Obviously, with this approach, as long as you put in place everything I've outlined above, especially your follow-up campaigns for each Expertise First Lead Magnet, you should be getting a huge return on your investment in time (and money if you outsource).

Even if this activity only yields a dozen clients, that's a significant return.

But, you will need to supplement this activity with paid traffic, especially if you're looking to build and scale your business so you have dozens, even hundreds of clients. You'll do that using YouTube and LinkedIn advertising...

YouTube Advertising

Advertising on YouTube is right now the best platform you can advertise on in terms of the cost and the return it will bring you.

Before we delve further, here are some startling facts about YouTube (source: youtube.com/yt/press/statistics.html), which explain why it's a such a valuable platform for us all to use...

- YouTube was launched on 14 February 2005 by Steve Chen, Chad Hurley, and Jawed Karim. Now it is the second most visited website in the world (after Google, which owns YouTube).

- The very first YouTube video was uploaded on 23 April 2005.

- The total number of people who use YouTube – 1,300,000,000.

- 300 hours of video are uploaded to YouTube every minute!

- Almost 5 billion videos are watched on YouTube every single day.

- In an average month, eight out of ten 18–49 year-olds watch YouTube.

- Six out of ten people prefer online video platforms to live TV.

- The total number of hours of video watched on YouTube each month – 3.25 billion.

- The average number of mobile YouTube video views per day is 1,000,000,000.

- The average mobile viewing session lasts more than 40 minutes. This is up with more than 50% year-over-year.

- Female users are 38%, male 62%.

- User Percentage by Age: 18–24 – 11%; 25–34 – 23%; 35–44 – 26%; 45–54 – 16%; 50–64 – 8%; 65+ – 3%; unknown age – 14%.

- You can navigate YouTube in a total of 76 different languages (covering 95% of the internet population).

But what the stats don't really tell you is that, unlike the other large advertising platforms such as Facebook, Instagram and LinkedIn, etc., because YouTube has so much inventory (videos), they currently don't have enough advertisers to cover it. Therefore, the costs are still significantly lower.

Plus, as you can see from the statistics above, it doesn't matter what type of business your mentoring skills and expertise serve, a large percentage of them can be reached via YouTube.

Better still, and not many people are aware of this, YouTube doesn't charge the advertiser a single penny unless your video ad is watched by a viewer for over 30 seconds. In other words, you have up to 30 seconds of FREE advertising. If a viewer clicks on 'Skip Ad' at 29 seconds or less, you pay ZERO.

Just read that again.

No other advertising platform gives you this.

To help put this into context, let me show you the last four months results of our YouTube ad campaign. Ignore the scale of the numbers. We advertise globally, so the numbers are many times higher than yours will be. I'm just showing you these so you can get a handle on why YouTube is such a great platform right now...

- In the last four months 2,703,384 people were exposed to our ads.

- Of these, 402,083 watched at least 30 seconds of our ads (and as I said above, YouTube only charges you when someone watches your ad for more than 30 seconds).

- That means we ALSO had 2,301,301 video views as FREE exposure.

- More importantly, for every pound spent (invested) on YouTube advertising, we returned £1.19 and a further £0.98 in recurring revenue. You can do the maths – invest £100,000, get a return of £119,000 and a recurring monthly revenue of £98,000).

So, let's step back for a second. My advice is that you start showing your ads to people within say a 10-mile radius of your home or office (just as you did when targeting businesses showing growth intent previously).

Plus, YouTube allows you to set a daily budget for each campaign you run. So, are you going to throw hundreds of pounds, dollars or euros at it straight away? No, of course not, because now you know you should be using the 'Minimum Risk Formula'. Therefore, set your daily budget at, say, just ten to twenty-five pounds, dollars or euros, until you get traction and the campaign is conforming to the '1 For 1' principle.

Then, and only then, can you start to scale up.

I could write an entire book on YouTube advertising, and this book isn't the platform to do that. However, YouTube produce some excellent step-by-step tutorials on how to set up a successful campaign so you can do it yourself. Or, you can find an ad agency who you can work with to help you through the process.

Setting up a YouTube campaign is complex but, I can assure you, it's very worthwhile.

Think about it...

If you spend (invest) say a thousand pounds, dollars or euros in your first month and you acquire three mentoring clients at £/$/€400 a month, you've made your money back and the following month those three clients will bring in £/$/€1,200 ... and so on. Figure 5.30 shows a screenshot of one of our YouTube videos...

Figure 5.30: One of Our YouTube Ads
(you only pay if the viewer watches <u>more</u> than 30 seconds)

LinkedIn Advertising

LinkedIn is a social network for professionals. It's a business-to-business (B2B) paradise. That's why it's a great platform for you to advertise on to find your mentoring clients!

Here are a few statistics to whet your appetite (source: Microsoft Organisation)...

- There are 630 million LinkedIn users worldwide.

- 44% of LinkedIn users are women.

- 61 million LinkedIn users are senior-level influencers, and 40 million are in decision-making positions.

- LinkedIn is the #1 channel B2B marketers use to distribute content.

- LinkedIn makes up more than 50% of all social traffic to B2B websites and blogs.

- 91% of marketing executives list LinkedIn as the top place to find quality content.

- 80% of B2B leads come from LinkedIn vs. 13% on Twitter and 7% on Facebook.

- LinkedIn generates three times more conversions than Twitter and Facebook.

As you can see, LinkedIn is without a doubt the place to be for B2B marketers so, again, it's the perfect platform when looking for business mentoring clients, especially because of LinkedIn's targeting options and the data they provide.

You can show your ads only to your specified target market.

So, for example, let's say your perfect target market for your mentoring service is females aged 35–54 running their own digital marketing business with 2–10 employees based in Leicester (UK). Well, LinkedIn will allow you to target them exactly on that specific basis!

What does that mean?

It means LinkedIn shows your ads only to those people identified by your targeting criteria. It's perfect targeting if you're targeting B2B clients... and, of course, you are!

We've spent (invested) hundreds of thousands of pounds in LinkedIn advertising over the last five years. We've tested all their various advertising options, but two formats stand out in terms of their overall cost and return on investment...

I advise you to use only 'Text Ads' and 'Sponsored InMail'.

Text Ads show up on various pages, such as the homepage feed, profile page, inbox, company page and search results page, but will only show on desktop NOT mobile (one of their disadvantages). The image in figure 5.31 shows you examples of text ads on my homepage feed...

Figure 5.31: Text Ads On Homepage Feed

Text ads are very easy to set up, since you are restricted to just one image, 25 characters for the headline and just 75 characters for the description.

Sponsored InMail campaigns are slightly more complex, because you get far more editorial options. Sponsored InMails are delivered to the LinkedIn Inbox of your target market. But, what a lot of people don't know is that unlike conventional email that drops into your email inbox once they are sent, LinkedIn will only drop your Sponsored InMail when a LinkedIn user you're targeting is actually logged in to their LinkedIn account. This significantly increases results.

The image shown in figure 5.32 is from one of my dormant LinkedIn accounts. Notice the top Sponsored Ad (also shown in the feed) is one of our ads targeting potential business mentors...

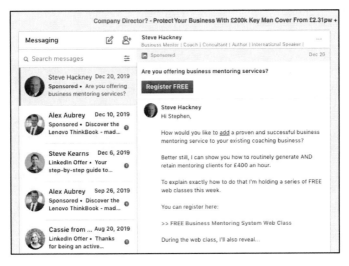

Figure 5.32: Sponsored Ads

Because of their simplicity, you definitely do NOT need an agency to help you set up a LinkedIn Text Ad or Sponsored InMail campaigns. Plus, just like YouTube, you can set a daily budget for your campaigns, so you never have to over-expose yourself financially.

***

Targeting businesses with growth intent, running a YouTube ad campaign and a LinkedIn ad campaign will ensure you never have to worry about where the next lead will come from, as long as you put in place everything we've described so far.

Systemising and Automating Your Lead Generation

All the previous elements regarding your lead generation have been developed with the overriding principle that once you have everything in place it will be completely systemised and automated.

This is the **KEY** to lead generation and, in fact, to building and scaling your mentoring business.

You want your 'Lead Generation System' to run 24/7, 365 days a year without you having to get involved in any part of it, other than, of course, putting everything in place and then tweaking it to improve results.

The diagram in figure 5.33 shows you a high-level view of how your Lead Generation System should look...

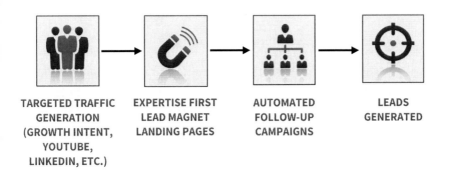

TARGETED TRAFFIC GENERATION (GROWTH INTENT, YOUTUBE, LINKEDIN, ETC.)   EXPERTISE FIRST LEAD MAGNET LANDING PAGES   AUTOMATED FOLLOW-UP CAMPAIGNS   LEADS GENERATED

Figure 5.33: High-Level View of a Lead Generation System

The entire system, when put in place correctly, should just keep running on autopilot, churning qualified leads out for you every week.

If it's not on autopilot, then I can tell you now that it's going to be really tough for you to grow your business. This is the system EVERY business should put in place, not just every mentoring business. It really is the secret to building a significant business.

So, make a promise to me and to yourself that following reading this book you'll start putting in place an actual 'Lead Generation System' that runs on autopilot. And, as long as you follow the steps I've laid out for you in this book, you'll do it and do it well.

Unfortunately, automation does, however, come at a cost in terms of the technology you need.

For example, this is what you'll need to ensure the whole system is automated...

- **Click Funnels** to build stunning landing pages...

  $297 per month

- **InfusionSoft (Keap)** for your CRM and follow-up campaigns (you can use Click Funnels for this, but it's still a little clunky and doesn't offer 'automated processes', which you'll need when it comes to working with your clients (see later)...

  $297 per month

- **Online Diary System** for your leads to book meetings with you...

  $6.50 per month

Therefore, at the very least, you'll need to budget for around $300 a month for your technology. But I promise you this is a drop in the ocean compared to what it will do for you and your business when set up properly.

Okay, you're moving fast now! Your Lead Generation System is in place, is fully automated, and it's generating a constant stream of leads for you, but that's only half the job done...

What you now need to do is make sure you convert as many of those leads into *mentoring clients at the **RIGHT** fee*. You do that with a 'Sales Conversion System'. It's really easy to put in place, and in the next chapter I'll take you through the exact steps you need to implement...

Chapter Summary

- The generation of leads is a very important part of your mentoring business and takes commitment, effort and hard work to put everything in place.

- There are only three types of media channels: E-Media, Published Media and Direct Marketing Media. There are numerous strategies within each media channel. Only choose the strategies where you know your target market can be reached.

- When it comes to generating leads, you should always use the principle of 'Expertise First'. That means before you try to sell your mentoring services, you should provide your prospect with a demonstration of your skills and expertise.

- There are four primary 'Expertise First Lead Magnets' (a lead magnet is something of value that is desired by your target market that you offer usually for free to them)...

  1. Critique
  2. Webinar
  3. Software Diagnostic Solution
  4. Monthly Printed Newsletter

- You must apply at least one Expertise First Lead Magnet to the front end of your Lead Generation System. The more, the better!

- To quickly build and scale your mentoring business, you'll use the principle of '1 For 1'. That means if you spend one pound, dollar or euro, on your lead generation activities, you get at least one pound, dollar or euro back. THIS IS ARGUABLY THE SINGLE BIGGEST PRINCIPLE YOU NEED TO MASTER.

- Always adhere to the 'Minimum Risk Formula'. This approach will ensure you minimise your losses and maximise your return when running marketing and advertising campaigns. Test small. Always.

- You shouldn't use numerous lead generation tactics and strategies. Select a couple and master them.

- The best three lead generation tactics to use to generate an abundance of leads are Growth Intent, YouTube advertising and LinkedIn advertising.

- Once a lead is generated, you must follow-up on it using SMS and email (and direct mail).

- When all the different elements of your Lead Generation System have been created and implemented you must systemise and automate it using technology such as Click Funnels and InfusionSoft (Keap).

CHAPTER 6:

ACQUIRING CLIENTS

$$R \times M \times L \times \underline{A} \times M$$

When I was thinking of joining Leicester Tigers, something happened that has stayed with me forever. It's a valuable story that you can benefit from right now, too.

I was at work when Michelle, our receptionist, called me to say a chap by the name of Tony Russ was on the phone. A year earlier, whilst still at Loughborough University, I had played for England Students, where Tony was the coach, so I knew him well. Tony, as I said previously, was also head coach at Tigers and the first-ever full-time, fully paid coach in world rugby. I had no idea why he was calling.

He said, "Steve, I'll cut to the chase. I've obviously seen you playing for Nottingham, and we worked more closely together with England Students last season. I want you to come to Leicester Tigers." (I'm only a 'prospect' at this stage.)

That conversation started the ball rolling in terms of me leaving Nottingham.

Tony asked me to think about it, which I did. He said he'd call back in a week, once I'd had time to think about it.

And, what happened next is one of the most valuable lessons I've ever had when it comes to nurturing leads and converting them into clients.

When Tony called back (as he promised he would!) I told him I was interested (I'm a 'lead' now), but I had some doubts and a lot of questions. He replied, "Look Steve, why don't you come to the Club where we can chat over lunch and I can answer any questions you have."

About a week later I went to see Tony but, prior to the meeting, Tony sent me an agenda. It detailed everything we would be covering. It was very impressive. It included a tour around the ground and the facilities, the vision of the Club, and various other things.

When we met, it was at this point that Tony talked about building a team that would rival the best in Europe. And, what really impressed me in addition was that Tony had organised various key people at the Club to join us at different times throughout the meeting. First, Peter Wheeler, Club Chairman and legend of the sport met with me to reinforce what Tony was saying. Then, Les Cusworth popped in to talk about me joining the Club and what it would do for my game (as you know, I would subsequently work with Pete and Les at P&G Bland). At the time, Les was also assistant England coach (to Jack Rowell), and I knew him well, as we had played together a few years before, for the Midlands, plus, of course, I was also in the England setup. Les told me in no uncertain way how much it would help my game if I joined Tigers.

And then Dean Richards turned up. Dean was captain of the first team and a Tigers and England superstar. Dean was a policeman at the time (remember, rugby union wouldn't turn professional for another five years). He came into Tony's office in his police uniform and again told me how much the Club wanted me and what he and Tony were looking to put in place.

Dean took me on a tour of the ground (which was very impressive). It was, and still is, one of the finest rugby stadiums on the planet. As an ambitious rugby player, it was impossible not to be impressed. Back then rugby was a much smaller sport than it is now. The average crowd for the likes of Nottingham (where I was playing) and Bath, then the top English Premiership teams, was around five or six thousand. Tigers would regularly get twelve to fifteen thousand. In terms of atmosphere when you are playing, I can tell you firsthand that the difference that seven thousand makes is huge.

Back then, Tigers' training facilities were like every other rugby club: poor. In fact, their gym was the size of a postage stamp and housed under one of the stands. But Tony showed me the plans of their new training facility at Oval Park. It was a standalone training facility about five miles from the stadium, destined in twelve months to become the finest rugby union training facility in the world. It included a state-of-the-art gym, all-weather pitches, and so on. Whereas this type of facility is commonplace, now, back then Tigers were at the forefront of player development. Tony reeled off the coaching team he had assembled, including the dieticians, speed coaches and so on. Remember, whilst having a support team like this is part of professional rugby, now, back then this approach was revolutionary. It was way ahead of its time and even legions ahead of football (soccer), which had been a professional sport in the UK for decades. Yet when it came to player development and training, soccer was simply back in the dark ages.

It was impossible for me not to be extremely impressed.

Then Tony said, "Steve, obviously this is not just your decision. I know Helen (Helen was my girlfriend at the time, but Tony had met her during our England Student games) needs to be comfortable with the Club, too." Again, this may not seem such a big thing, but I can tell you back then rugby was such a male-dominated sport (thankfully, it's not now) that for someone to even consider one's partner in the decision-making process was nigh on revolutionary! Tony went on to ask, "Steve, can we organise to bring Helen to the Club and show her around, too?"

What Tony was doing was making sure all the relevant decision-makers (stakeholders) were being considered.

It was a highly impressive 'courtship', and because of what Tony planned and the people he brought in to meet me, it demonstrated to me that they really cared about the players, their wives or partners, and that THEY WANTED ME.

After that process, it was simply impossible to say 'no'.

Was this a one-off? No, it wasn't. As I said earlier, prior to rugby turning professional, I progressed to running the marketing for the Club. And a big part of that role was player recruitment. Remember, we couldn't offer money, so we had to use the facilities of the Club, the coaching setup and, later, the training facilities as incentives for every player the Club was interested in... and, of course, we would set things up as Tony had done so skilfully with me.

That approach was responsible for building one of the finest rugby teams ever assembled, and one that would go on to dominate European and English club rugby for the best part of 20 years.

In fact, this was one of the best examples of what Dan Kennedy (the great US marketing strategist) calls 'Sales Choreography'.

Tony had put in place a number of powerful steps that he knew would have a major effect and influence on my decision-making process. From the first phone call, then the impactful agenda, right through to getting Helen involved in the decision-making process... it was all beautifully choreographed. And, remember, I would be joining a Club who already had three *England* wingers playing in 'my' position (Tony and Rory Underwood and Barry Evans)... so there was a significant risk that I'd struggle to get a game for the first team! Yet Tony, without making any promises, told me that if I kept improving my game as anticipated by him and his team of coaches, then there was no reason why I couldn't command a regular first-team place (which ultimately happened). But of course, I wasn't to know that at the time! I promise you, it was a huge risk for me.

And the type of approach that Tony had put in place to 'convert' me is exactly what you need to do when it comes to converting your leads into sales.

Put a series of steps in place that makes it impossible for the prospect NOT to become a client.

Very simply, you need a process that starts the moment the lead is generated and finishes once they become a client.

I call this a *'Sales Conversion System'*.

Once again, this is missing from almost every business, and I have never seen any business mentor or coach with a fully choreographed Sales Conversion System in place.

The good news is that everything up to this point has been done to make your system easy to put in place and to function very effectively.

We started right at the beginning of the book emphasising that you having a results-producing system is the foundation of your business. THAT'S REALLY IMPORTANT WHEN IT COMES TO ACQUIRING CLIENTS.

Then, we described putting in place your M.A.P. (Mentoring Attraction Package) so your mentoring service is highly desirable and packed full of value. THAT'S REALLY IMPORTANT WHEN IT COMES TO ACQUIRING CLIENTS.

Then we looked at putting in place your Expertise First Lead Magnets. THAT'S REALLY IMPORTANT WHEN IT COMES TO ACQUIRING CLIENTS.

So, although you may not have realised this at the time, we've been systematically setting everything up to make it so much easier for you to acquire clients and convert as many leads as possible.

But it's NOT just about acquiring the client. What's arguably more important is acquiring the client at the *RIGHT* fee... and, again, everything we've put in place up to this point has been with that in mind. It doesn't take skill to give your expertise away cheaply. The skill is to get clients at the fee(s) that YOU want.

And that's why I've taken the time so far to give you the platform for achieving that.

Let me take you through the Sales Conversion System you need to put in place.

Figure 6.1 shows the simple high-level view of it (remember, it needs to start the moment the lead is generated... and finish only once the client is acquired at the right fee).

What you'll see is that the cost to put in place your Sales Conversion System is negligible, but the results it will achieve for you will be astounding.

Every step you put in place should be systemised, then as much of it as possible should be automated. Of course, unless you're running an evergreen webinar (as described earlier), your 'online meeting' can't be automated, because you'll be doing that one-to-one in a live environment, but most of the other steps can and should be automated.

In time, you'll be able to build upon the system, and then tweak it so it produces the best possible results for you. Remember, the goal is simple...

To convert as many leads as you can into clients at the right fee. This is not rocket science, but it IS a science...

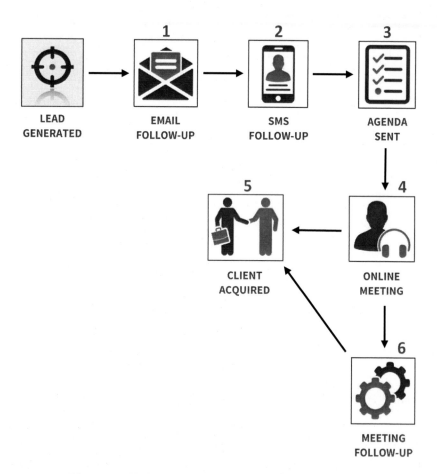

Figure 6.1: High-Level View of a Sales Conversion System

Let's go through each step…

STEP #1: Email Follow-Up

As soon as the lead is generated you should acknowledge this by sending them an email. This should be automated.

Here's an example, using our Scientific Marketing Makeover…

Subject: ~Contact.FirstName~ thank you…

Hi ~Contact.FirstName~

Thank you for requesting a <u>FREE</u> *Scientific Marketing Makeover*.

All you need to do now is send me your marketing piece, and I'll get working on it. Simply reply to this email and attach it to the email.

Remember, your Marketing Makeover can be on any sales and marketing piece you currently use.

My recommendation is for you to send me the piece that is costing you the most money at the moment (such as an advert, or a landing page/website where you are directing your traffic).

…but the choice is yours.

It usually takes around 48 hours for me to complete the Makeover, although I have recently had a large influx of Makeovers to complete, so please allow 72 hours.

Once I've completed the Makeover, I'll contact you to arrange an online meeting where I will take you through the improvements that will transform your strategy for **ZERO extra cost**.

Thanks again ~Contact.FirstName~.

To your success,

Full Name | *Business Growth Mentor*

P.S. If you haven't done so already, I urge you to request a **FREE** *Sales Accelerator ROADMAP analysis*. This ingenious software uses a special algorithm to fix your marketing and pinpoint the gaps in your sales and marketing where the quickest and biggest improvements can be made. It then provides a step-by-step ROADMAP on what to implement first, second, third... and so on. You can get all the details here...
>> FREE Sales Accelerator ROADMAP - FULL Details

STEP #2: SMS Follow-Up

Backup your email with an automated SMS. Here's an example...

Thank you for requesting a Scientific Marketing Makeover. I've just sent you an email which details the next steps. Thanks again.

STEP #3: Agenda Sent

Prior to the meeting, email an agenda (see example in figure 6.2).

STEP #4: Online Meeting

Your meeting should take place using an online meeting platform (Skype, GoTo Meeting, WebinarJam, Zoom, etc.). Do NOT waste time meeting the prospect in person (unless they are a close friend or colleague).

The really good news is that we covered most of this when building your webinar script.

Sales Accelerator ROADMAP
Online Meeting
Agenda

DETAILS:			
Company Name:	Enter client's business name	**Attendees:**	Client's name and Your name
Date of Meeting:	Enter date of meeting	**Time:**	Start and finish time (75 mins)

1. Introduction
2. The ROADMAP Analysis
3. Results
4. Questions
5. Next Steps

ACTIONS	WHO?	WHEN?

 The **Core Asset**

Figure 6.2: Meeting Agenda

This is what I recommend you do in terms of 'systemising' the meeting...

1. Introduce yourself and explain your story (I took you through this earlier when building your webinar script – see 'Stage 3 – Explain 'Your Story').

2. Then seamlessly move onto delivering your lead magnet.

3. Segue into your M.A.P. (see Stage 7 of the webinar script). Use the presentation slides already created for your webinar.

4. Next, reveal each value element of your M.A.P. (see Stage 8 of the webinar script).

5. Then simply follow the webinar script from Stage 10 and right through and including up to the end of Stage 15.

If you decide NOT to run a webinar, then you simply follow the steps outlined above to create your meeting script. If you follow the stages outlined, you'll have a very powerful and persuasive 'pitch'. And as long as you deliver a great lead magnet (which you will!) your prospect should be eating out of your hand by the end of the meeting.

...but you do have to practice... and practice your online meeting!

Bob Dwyer, one of my Leicester Tigers coaches, had a brilliant insight into player and personal improvement. He beautifully upgraded the often-used adage of 'Practice Makes Perfect' to '*Perfect* Practice Makes Perfect'.

When he first said that to us, I thought it was genius (and still do!).

What he wanted to get across with crystal clarity was that it's not practice that makes perfect... you have to get as close as possible to replicate match conditions in your practice and then you'll improve exponentially.

And, of course much of our training was done in as close to match conditions as we could without risking injury. Nevertheless, we often had full-on contact sessions (I used to hate these, by the way!), which regularly ended up with pitch battles, especially with the forwards (the big ugly blokes in the scrum!). In particular, Richard Cockerill and Neil Back would regularly fight during training sessions, and most people couldn't resist (teasingly) hitting Austin Healey... although he's a top bloke!

Anyway, the point I want to make is you should, of course, in the beginning practice your script a couple of times yourself, but then ask friends, colleagues and family members (ideally only those with businesses) if you could take them through your meeting.

This is as close as you'll get to 'perfect practice makes perfect', and I can assure you, it will pay you back many times.

I can tell you that most people don't do this. The first time they deliver their online meeting is with their first lead. That's plain stupid. You'll never get the results you could if you don't invest in proper practice. Preparation comes under a wider topic I call, 'Giving the Mentoring Industry the Respect It Deserves' and I'll talk more about this later.

STEP #5: Client Acquired

At the end of the online meeting it is very important that you 'close the sale' and ask for the order.

Despite what you may think, this is not pushy. This is not 'salesy'. You absolutely, categorically must ask the prospect to join your mentoring programme. They even EXPECT it.

Do not shy away from it.

Zig Ziglar, the great sales trainer and motivational speaker insightfully quoted, "Timid salesmen have skinny kids."

I love that. What he means is that if you don't ask for the order, you're not going to get many clients. You have to ask them to join your mentoring programme at the end of EVERY online meeting.

It's COMPULSORY.

However, even if you've followed everything so far, we don't live in a perfect world. So, whilst many people will become clients at the end of the online meeting, others won't.

They'll genuinely want to think about it. And there are a multitude of reasons why they may not want to go ahead right now. We covered this off as much as we could with your script in terms of the questions at the end of your meeting. In many respects, the questions are trying to overcome any potential reasons why the prospect won't go ahead right now but, nevertheless, it is, of course, unrealistic to think you'll close every meeting with a new client.

However, there is a contingency for this...

STEP #6: Meeting Follow-Up

If the prospect doesn't convert into a client at the meeting, then your 'Meeting Follow-Up' campaign begins.

Once again this should be a step-by-step system using a series of emails, SMS and direct mail.

One great tactic to use (and I've used this for many years) is to ask a series of maybe three or four questions in relation to what the prospect is doing within your area of expertise.

For example, let's say your expertise is in building profitable teams, and you would ask, say, three questions that focus on three individual areas of building profitable teams. For instance...

Do your staff each have individual KPIs (key performance indicators)?

Have you put in place a vision, mission, objectives, tactics and strategies policy together and communicated it to your team?

Do you carry out staff appraisals every six months?

(If your lead magnet is a diagnostic, you'll simply be able to take one of the 'No' answers the prospect provides and do what follows next...)

You obviously note down their answer and then, if at the end of the meeting that prospect didn't convert, you can then use this information as ammunition to help convert them.

Let's say when you asked the question, *"Does your staff each have individual KPIs (key performance indicators)?"*, they reply "No".

You can then write to them (don't use email for this, it won't give you the best result), thanking them for their time, reinforce the value elements of your mentoring programme, and then also enclose a step-by-step guide to how they can get their team to set individual KPIs. You're in effect giving them a VALUABLE BUT FREE GIFT that (also) reinforces your expertise. This is very powerful and will often help convert prospects who are 'sat on the fence'!

Are you starting to see all the pieces of the puzzle coming together? Everything, and I mean everything, you're doing is making getting clients at the right fee as easy as possible for you.

So, the great news is you now have a new client.

Next, you need to make sure you retain them for as long as possible and maximise the value of the relationship.

This is where 'Maximising Client Value' takes over... first, let's summarise what we've just covered.

Chapter Summary

- Generating an avalanche of leads is irrelevant if you don't have a process to convert as many of them as possible into clients at the right fee.

- It doesn't take skill to give your expertise away cheaply! Your goal is to acquire clients at the RIGHT fee.

- Put in place a 'Sales Conversion System' to increase client acquisitions.

- Remember, and act on, "*Perfect* Practice Makes Perfect".

- At the end of every online meeting you should ALWAYS ask for the order (ask the prospect to join your mentoring programme).

- Not every lead will convert into a client at the end of each online meeting. For those that don't, implement your follow-up campaign with them.

CHAPTER 7:

MAXIMISING CLIENT VALUE

$$R \times M \times L \times A \times \underline{M}$$

In my last season at Tigers I picked up a very bad groin injury that required surgery. The professional term for the injury is 'Gilmore's Groin'. It was named after the surgeon who invented a type of surgery that fixed the problem. Until then, sportsmen and women who had the injury would have to retire. Basically, the constant changing of direction common amongst footballers, basketball players and rugby players would with some people result in one of the muscles around the groin area literally ripping clean apart. It was agony.

Prior to Gilmore, there was no way of stitching the muscle back together with long-lasting effect. Gilmore invented a special gauze and mesh-like material that he would attach to both ends of the torn muscle and, over a period of just six weeks, the fibres in the muscle would grow around the gauze creating a solid bond (well that's what I was told!).

I had the surgery and, sure enough, after six weeks of rehab I was back to fitness and could start full training.

Unfortunately, I couldn't fully regain my biggest attribute, my speed and, at the top level of elite sport, even just a 1% decrease can make all the difference. Truth was, I knew it was time to quit!

However, out of the blue I received a call from my agent Simon Cohen. He told me he'd been speaking to the owners of a club in the division below the Premiership who had significant investment and were looking to build a squad good enough to get promotion into the Premiership. They wanted a mix of young and experienced players. Simon told them I was considering retiring, but they asked if they could speak with me with the intention of persuading me to not hang my boots up, just yet.

To cut a long story short, I knew I didn't have the speed to play at the highest level, but one league down would be fine. I passed my fitness test and began life for the first time in the Second Division.

At the time, I really was hell bent on retiring, but Moseley Rugby Club (based in Birmingham) offered me £45,000 a year for three years, part-time. It meant I could concentrate on building my business as I had done at Tigers, and still get paid for doing what I loved.

I was going from a world-class club to (with respect) a second-rate club, but one with big ambitions. In fact, in the 1970s Moseley were one of the biggest clubs in England and wanted to bring back past glories. So, they did have a successful history.

I, of course, had reservations but, as with everything I do, I went into it 110%. I did all the press and TV interviews prior to the first training session. Then we trained.

To be honest I was pleasantly surprised with the quality of the training (the coach was Alan Lewis. He had coached Wales and knew what he was doing, although we never gelled). And on the plus side, my groin was feeling fine.

Then, after training we went back into the training rooms, stripped off and went into the showers. I turned the shower on and kept turning and turning the tap, but all that came out was a trickle. I went to the next shower... and the next... and the same thing. The showers were pathetic. I knew right at that instant I'd made a terrible mistake.

I should have retired.

You're probably wondering why I came to this conclusion on the basis of the showers not working. Well, here's my thought process...

I'd been at a rugby club (Tigers) who put the players (their clients) at the heart of the club. Everything they did was with the players' development and welfare in mind. How they treated us, and our wives and partners, was world-class in every way.

When I turned on those showers at Moseley, I instantly knew I'd joined a club that didn't have that same philosophy. If they can't even spend the money (which wasn't a lot) to make sure the showers are working for the players, what else weren't they doing when it came to player development and welfare.

As it turned out, it was a disaster. My worst fears were realised at every junction. I joined in the August, and I was sacked in December, as they ran out of money and needed to cut their more expensive players.

So, what's the point of this story, I hear you ask?

Quite simply, you'll never create a world-class mentoring business (the essence of this book, remember!) unless you focus on and treat your clients in a world-class way.

Figuratively speaking, even the little things like the showers need to be world-class. Otherwise, you won't retain your clients for long, and you won't ethically maximise your earnings from them.

It's simple... don't have any 'broken showers' in your mentoring business!

Broken showers are visible in many businesses. We've all experienced them before.

Therefore, this chapter focusses on making sure you don't have any 'broken showers' in your business and what to do to maximise income with your clients.

To begin this crucial phase, let me set the scene by taking you through a brilliant concept called 'Moments Of Truth' that will ensure you never have a single broken shower in your business...

Using Moments of Truth to Wipe Out 'Broken Showers' and Create a World-Class Client Experience

In 1987, Jan Carlzon, the CEO of Scandinavian Airlines, wrote the book *Moments of Truth*. It explained how he took the airline from deficit to profit by 'moving' the airline to a world-class customer-focussed organisation.

Now, as you know, there have been many books written on customer service, but where this book and Carlzon's strategies really differ is his focus on each individual interaction the customer has with the business. He calls these ***Moments of Truth***, and, of course, each interaction can be a positive or a negative experience.

Take a look at the diagram shown in figure 7.1. It shows how, at each contact (Moment of Truth), you need to ensure each interaction is a favourable one for the customer. For instance, the broken showers at Moseley Rugby Club are a Moment of Truth.

Scandinavian Airlines prospered because they worked very hard to make sure each Moment of Truth with their customers was a very positive experience, and the results they achieved were a testament to this.

Therefore, what you need to do is increase the satisfaction level of each client when any point of contact (Moment of Truth) occurs. A point of contact can be a meeting (online or offline), a letter/postcard, SMS, email, telephone call, etc., in fact, any way in which your business comes into contact with a client.

So, how can you use this to your advantage? There are just a couple of simple steps. Let's take a look at each one...

Moments of Truth Explained

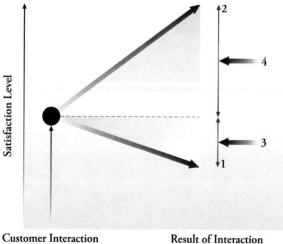

Legend

1. The effect on the customer when the business doesn't actively focus on each interaction with its customers. Notice the Moment of Truth was a negative experience, reducing the customer's satisfaction and therefore creating discontent (no matter how small).

2. Moments of Truth approach. By breaking down each point of contact to ensure excellent customer experience, the interest and satisfaction level is raised even higher.

3. Shows the drop in interest level and satisfaction when a business doesn't focus on each point of contact.

4. Shows the increase gained by using Moments of Truth.

Figure 7.1: Moments of Truth

Write Down All Possible Interactions (Moments of Truth) You Have With Your Clients.

This is simple. Here's what you do...

Use the 'Moments of Truth Design Table' (see figure 7.2) and first identify every single interaction you have with your clients and enter them in the 'Moment of Truth' column – every single one. Write these in chronological order (where possible).

Then, for each section, make sure you enter *when* the moment will happen and the detail of *what* you'll be doing to make it a positive experience for the customer.

Notice there are four sections.

Section 1: Client Acquired – Immediate Moments (in here, write down exactly what happens the moment you get a client).

For example...

- 'Thank-You Email' sent
- 'Thank-You SMS' sent

Section 2: Mentoring Service Delivery Moments (in here, write down the points of contact as you deliver your mentoring service to the client).

For example...

- Email meeting agenda (as per the Business Mentoring System)
- Send reminder SMS (as per the Business Mentoring System).
- Start the online meeting on time.

MOMENT OF TRUTH	WHEN
MENTORING CLIENT ACQUIRED – IMMEDIATE MOMENTS	
MENTORING SERVICE DELIVERY MOMENTS	
ONGOING MOMENTS	
SPECIAL MOMENTS	
WORLD-CLASS CLIENT EXPERIENCE AND NO 'BROKEN SHOWERS'!	

Figure 7.2: Moments of Truth Design Table

- Follow the Business Mentoring System to deliver a world-class meeting.

Section 3: Ongoing Moments (in here, write down the things you're going to do to keep in touch with the client).

For example..

- Send email mid-month making sure the client is getting on with their tasks.

Section 4: Special Moments (in here, write down things you're going to do that will WOW the client).

In the first three sections you've added only the basics, but they are still very important. This is the minimum level of positive interaction you should be having with your clients.

Without question, when you adopt Moments of Truth, you'll be adding so much more to each section. We do this with *Special Moments of Truth*. For example, here's what I'd add:

Section 1 – Special Moments:

What I'm going to reveal to you now will set you apart, not just from virtually every other mentoring, coaching and consulting business in the world, but from 99.9% of all businesses.

Once you get a new mentoring client, after sending the 'Thank-You Email' and 'Thank-You SMS', you should mail them what I call a 'Welcome Pack' (see the images shown in figure 7.3).

It's essential you send this by post (i.e. not digitally) to guarantee maximum effect.

Figure 7.3: The Welcome Pack

What you do is get a mailing box designed in your branding with the name of your mentoring programme on the front.

Believe me, when this is delivered, your clients will be astounded, and it reassures them that they've joined a world-class programme and mentor.

Inside the box, add a letter welcoming them to your mentoring programme and include any other elements that add to the value of it. For example...

- Company-branded merchandise (as you can see, we add two branded stress balls, the inference being that with our mentoring programme the client will lose stress as they build their business).

- Video testimonials from clients on a memory stick (for example).

- Your book, or a book from an author that compliments your work (as you can see, we include my 'FORMULA' book).

- A copy of your latest issue of your newsletter.

- And anything else you can think of that will make your new client think 'WOW!'

Believe me, this will create an amazing first impression of you and your mentoring programme. Don't think about doing it... just do it!

Section 2 – Special Moments:

- Every time there is a significant result for the client, send them a 'Congratulations Gift'. The first gift should be a bottle of champagne! You'll be surprised how much difference this makes!

Section 3 – Special Moments:

- Send your monthly printed newsletter.

This is NOT rocket science. We all instinctively know what will make people think 'WOW', because we're all customers of many other businesses. We can also count on one hand how many businesses we've bought from which make us think 'WOW'.

Another Great Example of Moments of Truth From an Unexpected Industry

Just in case you have any doubts about the power of Moments of Truth and the effect they can have on your mentoring business, here's a great example from an unexpected industry – a cab (taxi) company (and… if they can do it so can you!)…

Harvey Mackay (author of *Swim with the Sharks Without Being Eaten Alive*), tells a wonderful story about a cab driver that demonstrates Moments of Truth perfectly.

Harvey was waiting in line for a ride at the airport.

When a cab pulled up, the first thing Harvey noticed was that the taxi was polished to a bright shine.

Smartly dressed in a white shirt, black tie and freshly-pressed black slacks, the cab driver jumped out and rounded the car to open the back passenger door for Harvey.

He handed Harvey a laminated card and said:

'I'm Wally, your driver. While I'm loading your bags in the trunk, I'd like you to read my mission statement.'

Taken aback, Harvey read the card. It said: Wally's Mission Statement:

To get my customers to their destination in the quickest, safest and cheapest way possible in a friendly environment.

This blew Harvey away, especially when he noticed that the inside of the cab matched the outside: spotlessly clean!

As he slid behind the wheel, Wally said, 'Would you like a cup of coffee? I have a thermos of regular and one of decaf.'

Harvey said, jokingly, 'No, I'd prefer a soft drink.'

Wally smiled and said, 'No problem. I have a cooler up front with regular and Diet Coke, water and orange juice.'

Almost stuttering, Harvey said, 'I'll take a Diet Coke.'

Handing him his drink, Wally said, 'If you'd like something to read, I have the *Wall Street Journal, Time, Sports Illustrated* and *USA Today*.'

As they were pulling away, Wally handed Harvey another laminated card.

'These are the stations I get and the music they play if you'd like to listen to the radio.'

And, as if that were not enough, Wally told Harvey that he had the air conditioning on and asked if the temperature was comfortable for him.

Then he advised Harvey of the best route to his destination for that time of day.

He also let him know that he'd be happy to chat and tell him about some of the sights or, if Harvey preferred, to leave him with his own thoughts.

Then Harvey said, 'Tell me, Wally, have you always served customers like this?'

Wally smiled into the rear-view mirror. 'No, not always. In fact, it's only been in the last two years. My first five years driving, I spent most of my time complaining like all the rest of the cabbies do.

'Then I decided to do things differently. I looked around at the other cabs and their drivers. The cabs were dirty, the drivers were unfriendly, and the customers were unhappy. So I decided to make some changes. I put in a few at a time. When my customers responded, well, I did more.'

'I take it that has paid off for you,' Harvey said.

'It sure has,' Wally replied. 'In my first year, I doubled my income from the previous year. This year I'll probably quadruple it. You were lucky to get me today. I don't sit at cabstands anymore.

'My customers call me for appointments on my cell phone or leave a message on my answering machine. If I can't pick them up myself, I get a reliable cabbie friend to do it, and I take a piece of the action.'

Wally was implementing Moments of Truth, even though he didn't realise it!

This true story shows if Moments of Truth can be so successful for a cab driver, it can work for YOU!

The Four Sectors to Maximise Client Value

Okay, so we've ensured the client experience with you is amazing. We've also ensured you'll never have any 'broken showers'.

Don't underestimate how important this is. Adding Moments of Truth to your mentoring business catapults it to world-class status in a heartbeat.

Now, what we need to do is capitalise on the relationship you're building with each mentoring client and to maximise your revenue from them. This really is a weak area in most mentoring and coaching businesses, yet it's so easy to do.

I call this 'Maximising Client Value'. There are four ways to do so...

1. **Increase the frequency of purchase** (getting clients to buy more often).

2. **Increase referrals** (getting clients to recommend you more often).

3. **Increase average order value** (increasing the value of every sale).

4. **Reduce attrition** (keeping clients longer).

As I mentioned earlier, it's also important you implement each tactic or strategy as quickly as you can to ensure you maximise your results to the full.

This is a very exciting part of building your mentoring business. There are so many easy tactics and strategies you can add.

The good news is that you've already added Moments of Truth, which is great, because it has a major effect on all four areas above.

So, what I'm going to do now is to take you through the key strategies for each of the four areas, starting with 'Increasing The Frequency of Purchase'...

Frequency of Purchase: Continuity in Advance

If you recall, when I first started out, I would copy what other coaches and consultants at the time were doing. When it came to billing the client I would invoice them monthly, but only at the end of the month. So, for example, if I started working with a client on 1 September, I would send an invoice at the end of September for them to pay.

In almost every case, the payment wouldn't arrive for at least 2–4 weeks. Worse still, occasionally some clients wouldn't pay. That meant I was working for FREE.

Operating your business this way is plain stupid. And I quickly learned that it's crazy to work before getting paid. Yet that's still how most people do it!

So, lesson one is to never do any work _before_ being paid.

Simply tell the new client how you work in terms of billing and that you bill in advance. Then there are no surprises. As soon as their first payment is made, you commence working together. Pretty simple!

Next you should _not_ be providing a one-off mentoring service. I appreciate the way we've set up your M.A.P. and everything else assumes a monthly commitment in terms of you providing your service, but just to emphasise the point, you should be selling your mentoring service once and once only so it runs until the end of time or until you or the client wants to end the relationship.

This creates 'continuity'. That means every month your clients pay you in advance. If you have 10 clients each paying you £/$/€400 a month, then at the start of each month you earn £/$/€4,000. In other words, you're not starting from scratch every month. Business Mentoring lends itself to this approach but, since so few mentors and coaches take the initiative, it's important that I emphasise it for you.

Of course, you don't have to bill monthly. You could bill quarterly, every six months or even annually, _but the main lesson is to bill in advance_!

Increase Referrals: The Referral System

Many people fail to ask for referrals from existing clients. Just hoping and waiting for your best clients to refer friends, colleagues and business associates isn't good enough.

That approach is what I call 'passive'.

You're 'hoping' that providing a world-class mentoring service will translate into goodwill, and that clients will refer others to you.

Of course, every world-class business gets referrals, but if I told you that with very little additional cost you could multiply the referrals you get by a factor of five or ten, would you be interested?

Well, that's exactly what will happen when you put in place an effective *referral system.*

Putting in place a referral system that focuses on getting referrals is one of the easiest and most rewarding things you can do.

A structured referral system will give your business the following benefits:

- A constant supply of quality referrals.

- Increased enthusiasm dealing with people who are highly-interested in your mentoring service.

- An increase in the quality of mentoring clients.

- Increased profits. You spend less time and money when you acquire referred clients. They have already been recommended, so your cost-per-lead is zero, and since they've been recommended to you, their trust is already established.

- As a result, referred clients tend to value your mentoring service more than an 'ordinary' prospect. They usually don't 'shop around' meeting other mentors or coaches. This means you'll be able to sell your mentoring service at the RIGHT price, without quibble.

- A referral system will also help strengthen relationships with your clients. By helping their friends, colleagues and business associates, you make clients look good in the eyes of the referred party.

How to Get More Referrals

The key to getting more referrals is to offer an *effective* incentive. This one thing puts your referral system on steroids and will multiply results. It doesn't have to be a cash incentive. Tickets to a sporting occasion, the opera, cinema, a donation to your client's favourite charity... in fact, anything that the client values, are excellent ways of rewarding them. Remember, it doesn't cost you to acquire a referred client, so you can afford to give an incentive. Don't be tight! The bigger and more relevant the incentive, the more referrals you'll get. Fact!

Transform Your Mentoring Business into A Referral 'Machine'

You'll find it relatively easy to put a referral system in place. Choose your incentive, communicate the referral system regularly, and you're on your way. Results will be good, but you can improve them significantly by immersing the business in the referral system.

Here's what I mean:

Your referral system will help to create a constant stream of referrals, but that's not good enough.

Sure, it will bring you many more new clients than ever before, but you can turbo-charge your referral system by INTEGRATING it completely into your mentoring business. This is when you create your own 'Referral Mushroom', and your business transforms into a 'referral-based business'! The diagram in figure 7.4 shows you exactly what I mean by this, and what you should do.

So, let's look at what you need to do to integrate the system completely into your business.

Add to all agendas

The last item of your online meeting agenda should always be a reinforcement of your referral system.

When you get to this point in the agenda, reiterate to the client what your referral system involves (depending on the incentive you've chosen) and explain to them what they get as a result of a referral that converts into a client.

Tell them that your best clients are always referred ones, and that's why you invest so much time and effort in your referral programme.

Add to all emails

Reinforce your key referral message in your email signature by adding your referral incentive.

Add to bills/invoices

Another great place to reinforce your referral system is at the bottom of all your bills/invoices.

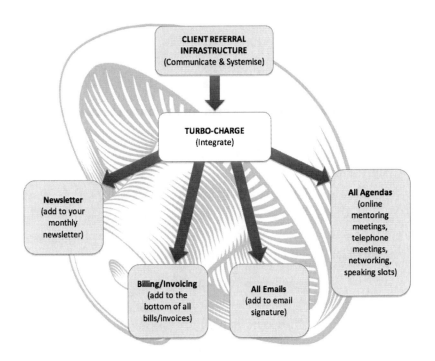

Figure 7.4: The Referral Mushroom

Add to your monthly newsletter

Adding your referral message to the bottom of each page in your monthly printed newsletter is a great way to reinforce your referral programme.

In fact, your newsletter is an excellent place to add case studies from clients who have referred other people to you.

Increasing the Average Order Value: Up-Sell and Cross-Sell

Up-selling and cross-selling are two of the easiest yet most neglected initiatives that can instantly add hundreds, thousands, even tens of thousands of pure profit to any mentoring business.

Perhaps the best way to explain an up-sell is to use a well-known up-sell that the food retailer McDonald's uses. Let's say you go into McDonald's and ask for any of their standard meals. The reply from the person serving you will be, 'Do you want to go large?' Basically, they are using a well-rehearsed *'Up-sell Statement'* that makes it easy for the buyer to say 'yes' (they also now use this same approach with their 'self-order terminals', only the prompt is displayed rather than spoken).

With just six carefully-crafted words, McDonald's generates an up-sell that 30%–40% of customers say 'yes' to! Yes, that's another 30–40 people in every hundred that spend, say, a pound more than they would have done had the Up-sell Statement not been used.

And just think for a moment ...

The cost to McDonald's for providing the larger-sized meal probably adds up to about 10p – so they've just created another 90p of profit on the sale with virtually no effort (six words).

To define up-sell more accurately:

An up-sell is when you move the client up to a larger quantity (bigger size, etc.) of the same mentoring service for a perceived preferential price.

For example, instead of one hour per month, you can up-sell your client to two or three hours and so on.

Let me now explain cross-selling. Let's use the McDonald's example again to demonstrate how the cross-sell works.

You go into McDonald's and ask for any of their main dishes, such as a Big Mac, or a Chicken Sandwich. The reply from the person serving you will be, 'Would you like fries with that?' Basically, they are using a well-rehearsed *'Cross-sell Statement'* that makes it easy for the buyer to say 'yes'.

To define cross-sell more accurately:

A cross-sell is when you sell a complimentary product or service to the mentoring service initially bought.

For example, you could make your software diagnostic tool a standalone product that clients pay more for. Or, you could invite them into your group 'Mastermind' mentoring programme (see later).

So, why do the up-sell and cross-sell work so well?

The reason why they work so well is that the up-sell or cross-sell is used only after the person has made the decision to buy and become a client. That means they are comfortable with their decision. It's at this point they are much more susceptible to the up-sell or cross-sell, because they are in 'buying mode'.

You should be aiming to convert upwards of 30% of people with an up-sell or cross-sell.

Your Mastermind Group Programme

So far, we've only talked about you delivering your mentoring service 'one-to-one'. This is, of course, a great model, and it will serve you very well. However, you should also consider having a 'one-to-many' mentoring programme, too.

This would be your 'Mastermind Group'.

Putting a Mastermind Group in place is beyond the scope of this book, but I just wanted to alert you to the benefits a Mastermind Mentoring Programme will have for you, your clients and your business...

- By running a one-to-many programme you are significantly leveraging your time and income potential. For example, you could have 15 clients in your Mastermind group each paying you upwards of £/$/€500 per month. That means for, say, half a day's work each month you are making £/$/€7,500.

- You just have to facilitate each session and then provide your words of wisdom at relevant points. With a Mastermind approach, everyone in the group will offer suggestions and solutions, so you and everyone else in the group get the combined wisdom of everybody. This is why Mastermind groups are usually so successful.

- You'll also pick up so many tips and improvements that can be added to your programme as part of your continual development.

Once you've got your mentoring programme up and running with clients and, of course, its producing results, you'll be ready to add a Mastermind Group.

Let's now look at the last area for maximising client value: *Reducing Attrition...*

Reducing Attrition: Delivering Results

World-class businesses don't lose many clients. Unfortunately, we don't live in a perfect world, so you can't completely eliminate client attrition from your business, but much of what I've covered with you in this book will ensure you reduce client losses to a minimum. I still work with clients who have been with me for years, and there's no reason why you can't achieve this with many of your clients.

Without question, THE most important factor in retaining clients is *getting results for them.*

That's why I started with results as the foundation of your mentoring business. It's rare that you'll lose a client if you're getting results for them.

There are, of course, other elements to factor in, here, but if your primary focus is to achieve results for your clients and you succeed, you won't ever have an issue with customer attrition, and you'll retain 90% of your clients for many, many months, even years.

Chapter Summary

- If you absolutely minimise 'broken showers' (in other words, treating your clients poorly) your clients will love working with you and will happily keep buying from you.

- Maximising client value is an essential part of running your mentoring business.

- There are just four key areas to maximise client value:

  1. Increase the frequency of purchase
  2. Increase referrals
  3. Increase the average order value
  4. Reduce attrition (client losses)

- Proven, low-cost strategies to maximise client value:

  1. Moments of Truth
  2. Continuity in Advance
  3. Referral System
  4. Provide More Time Per Month as an Easy Up-Sell
  5. Add a Mastermind Group
  6. Deliver Results

CHAPTER 8:

PUTTING IT ALL TOGETHER

Phew! That was some ride. I've taken you through the five key elements that will help you create a hugely successful mentoring business. I hope you have got a lot out of it, so far. But we're not finished yet!

Here's a recap of the 'Business Mentoring Success Equation':

$$R \times M \times L \times A \times M$$

$$=$$

Successful Mentoring Business

I've explained the importance of focussing on getting results for your clients. This is, without question, THE single most important factor that will determine your ultimate success.

To ensure clients get results, you've put in place two key systems: a business mentoring system for you to follow with each client and an implementation system for clients. Combined, these two systems will ensure clients get results.

Then we created a powerful M.A.P. (Mentoring Attraction Package) to add huge value to your proposition, making it so much easier to acquire clients at the right fee.

Next, we moved onto lead generation. You can't hide the fact that you have to spend (invest) money to acquire clients, but as long as you get close to the '1 For 1' principle (spend one pound, dollar or euro and get one pound, dollar or euro back), you'll be able to build and scale your mentoring business... and fast.

Then I described the merits of putting in place a sales conversion *system* which helps you to acquire more clients from the leads you generate.

And, finally, we discussed the importance of <u>maximising value</u> from all your clients.

Putting in place these five elements will ensure your success, but it WON'T actually give you a world-class mentoring business. You need one extra vital ingredient to make it happen...

Giving the Mentoring Industry the Respect It Deserves

Let me tell you a quick story that will help you appreciate what I mean by this...

Prior to rugby union turning professional in 1995, I had to work to put food on the table! If you recall, just prior to the game turning professional I was working in the insurance sector.

This is what my week looked like...

Monday to Thursday I would rise at 5 a.m. and drive to the club's training ground to train in the gym. Each session would last around 90 minutes. I'd then shower (good showers!), put my suit on, and drive to work. I'd arrive at work at 8 a.m. and would work hard until 12.45 p.m. I'd then leave work and drive to the track (which fortunately was a five-minute drive from the office). I'd then do a speed or speed endurance session with Merv Wilson (the club's speed coach). That session would last around 45 minutes. I'd then shower (again) and go back to the office and work hard until 6.30 p.m. (twice a week, this session would be replaced by my speed and agility training with Tim Exeter). I'd then drive to the club's training ground to train with the rest of the team. Training would finish at around 8.30 p.m., after which the club would provide us a cooked meal. I'd then drive home, spend an hour or so with Helen, and then go to bed (a little tired!).

Friday, I would rise at 6.30 a.m. and drive to the club for a massage and then drive to my office. Late Friday afternoon we'd have a team run through before the match on Saturday. On Saturday, I had a pre-match routine to get me physically and mentally ready for the match, and that routine was never to be disturbed. Helen wouldn't come anywhere near me on Saturdays ...until after the game! Then on Sunday I'd drive to the club and we'd do a team recovery session.

Then, the week's regime would start again!

I had a strict diet (which was structured to ensure I wouldn't lose any weight – when you're training that much you have to have a huge calorie intake – and, of course, to maximise my performance). I had to drink copious amounts of fluids and stock up on various minerals. And, I had to sleep well. That was my typical routine from the moment I graduated from Loughborough University until the game turned professional.

In reality, I (like my teammates) was a professional rugby player in every sense of the word, except I wasn't being paid as a 'professional' would have been.

It was 24/7, 334 days a year (three weeks off at the end of the season to recuperate – players get six weeks, now, and rightly so).

And it was no different when we went fully-professional. I packed my job in, but to be the very best at this level, you have to completely dedicate yourself and do *everything you can* to be the best (or try to be the best). In my experience, few people outside of elite sport experience this degree of desire and complete commitment so, let's say, at the very least you needed to be the best version of yourself.

It makes me laugh when people say, "I could have been a professional athlete." The reality is that very few people are able to give their sport (or their lives) this level of commitment. It doesn't matter how talented they are, if they don't commit 100%, they won't make it.

UNLESS THEY GIVE THE SPORT THE RESPECT IT DESERVES, THEY'LL NEVER SUCCEED.

And it's NO different when it comes to building a world-class mentoring business.

You can 'play' at this, or you can give it the respect it deserves.

What does that mean? Well, it means you never stop learning. And...

It means you dedicate yourself to being the best mentor you can be.

It means you attend training and workshops (online and offline) and digest and deploy the best learnings.

It means you read an outstanding business or self-improvement book every week.

It means you strive to improve every area of your business.

It means you prepare fully before every meeting.

It means you are continually looking to improve yourself.

(Oh, and just to mention quietly, that you are preoccupied by delivering awe-inspiring results for all of your clients!)

...and when you do that, the Business Mentoring Success Equation, changes to this (notice the added 'R' at the end)...

$$(R \times M \times L \times A \times M)R$$

$$=$$

World-Class and Highly Successful Mentoring Business

Sir David Brailsford who masterminded Great Britain's incredible cycling success at the last three Olympics, put their success down to 'marginal gains'. The team worked out that there were dozens of small performance elements related to both the athlete and the bikes they rode and that tweaking each of these only by small percentages would result in a big improvement.

And, if you think about it, your business is no different. If you imagine your business and yourself as a professional athlete, and you apply marginal gains by giving the industry the respect it deserves, what you're doing is creating a world-class business and transforming yourself into a world-class mentor.

Better still, because so few mentors and coaches genuinely give the industry the respect it deserves, it won't take you long before you're leaps and bounds ahead of your competition. I'm serious. And, I know, because I see so many examples!

We all need to help each other. Business mentoring is in the ascendancy and growing fast. It hasn't been tainted like business coaching and consultancy has... yet!

The reason why coaching and consulting has been tarnished is because there are too many coaches and consultants *not* giving the industry the respect it deserves.

So, do yourself, me and the rest of the mentoring industry a big favour and simply give it the respect it deserves. That will ensure we safeguard the huge benefits of business mentoring for decades to come and automatically give you a world-class business that will provide everything you ever wanted.

But, having said all that, I do know how difficult it is.

Where do you start? How do you take everything I've given you to build a world-class mentoring business and ultimately do everything within your power to give the industry the respect it deserves? I can tell you from hard-earned experience that it isn't easy. But there is an easier way... a far easier way, and that's what the last chapter focusses on...

Chapter Summary

- To build a world-class mentoring business you apply the 'Business Mentoring Success Equation' and then dedicate yourself to giving the mentoring industry the respect it deserves:

$$(R \times M \times L \times A \times M)R$$

$$=$$

World-Class and Highly Successful Mentoring Business

- By looking to improve every area of your business, then your own performance and development complimented by applying the concept of marginal gains, you'll be so far ahead of virtually everyone else in the industry.

CHAPTER 9:

YOUR SPECIAL INVITATION

I hope you've enjoyed this journey so far with me. I appreciate you may be feeling overwhelmed at the moment (there's a lot to take in), but if you apply just a fraction of what I've revealed to you in this book, you'll be on your way to creating a successful mentoring business.

However, in all my 20-plus years of mentoring and helping many hundreds of other people create successful mentoring businesses, it may surprise you to know there is ONE BIG PROBLEM which holds most back.

They don't have the resources (time and money) to put everything in place for each of the six elements.

As you might rightly surmise, it's taken me *years* to really understand exactly what's required to build a world-class mentoring business. And, to be frank, I could never have done it without the help, support, advice and added experience and expertise of Peter and Rob.

We've invested literally hundreds of thousands of pounds in developing our systems to ensure our mentors and their clients are successful... and, to find the right answers, we've made more mistakes than I care to remember (many of which I've mentioned in this book).

So, for you to get to this point, you can, of course, do it, but it will take considerable time, effort and investment.

But there is a low-cost and less time intensive solution...

It's called the **'Business Mentoring System'**.

Peter, Rob and I have basically taken everything detailed in this book (and much more) to create the world's largest and most successful community of business mentors.

We currently work with hundreds of people around the world supporting them in becoming world-class and highly successful *'Business Growth Mentors'*. In our programme, you get to 'bypass' the time, effort and cost of doing it on your own!

The Business Mentoring System comes with everything you need:

...to start, build and scale a world-class mentoring business. One where you'll be guiding and helping other business owners to achieve unparalleled success.

...and, from your viewpoint, the best thing about it is, we've done all the hard work for you.

If you recall, I explained earlier that if you automated your lead generation system, you would have to pay between $300 and $600 a month just for the technology.

However, with ZERO up-front licence or training fees and no exorbitant monthly support fees, you can have the entire Business Mentoring System for a *very special one-off incredibly affordable set-up fee*, with everything all completely tailored and personalised to you!

It's the complete solution for building and scaling a mentoring business. Other than your lead generation spend (investment), there are absolutely NO extra or hidden costs. The system even includes all of the technology costs, including your follow-up campaigns and landing pages!

I've created a special page where you can see everything included in the Business Mentoring System and the small investment required (you'll be pleasantly surprised). Here it is...

www.BusinessMentoringSystem.com/bms-book

Remember, follow the steps laid out in this book and give the mentoring industry the respect it deserves, and you'll be well on your way.

Thanks for spending your time with me and for investing in this book.

To your success,

Steve Hackney

P.S. Growing your mentoring business isn't rocket science, but it IS a science!

OTHER RESOURCES

Other Books Written By Steve

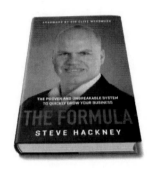

THE FORMULA – The Proven And Unbreakable System To Quickly Grow Your Business.

Get your FREE copy here (just pay a small shipping and handling fee)…

https://www.freeformulabook.com

Say 'Hi' on Social

LinkedIn: https://www.linkedin.com/in/stevehackney

Facebook: https://www.facebook.com/SteveTHackney

Twitter: https://twitter.com/SteveTHackney

Instagram: http://instagram.com/stevethackney

Pinterest: https://www.pinterest.com/SteveTHackney